ERP for Dummies

ERP for Dummies

Authored by
Ronnie Bishop, CPIM, CPM, CIERP
and Mary Ellen Lucas, CIERP

Edited by
Travis Anderegg, CFPIM, CIRM, CIERP
and Janice Knox, CIERP

Reviewed by

Resource Publishing
Eau Claire, WI

ISBN 0-9700352-2-5

Library of Congress Card Number: xx-xxxxxx

Printed and bound by Resource Publishing.

This book is dedicated to
All the people that wonder about the meaning of ERP.

▶ Meet Ronnie Bishop

Hi, my name is Ronnie Bishop. I chose to write this book because I have been asked numerous times, what is this thing called "ERP" and can it be explained in plain, simple terms.

As an ERP practitioner I have learned that failure to understand what ERP is and failure to understand the capabilities of the ERP system are 2 of the major reasons most companies fail to reap the full benefits of ERP. Far too often, software vendors, consultants, and educators tend to use terms that are unfamiliar or too technical for the everyday lay person. Their explanations sound like a lot of gobligook. I believe education and training should be based on practical, real-world information, presented in plain everyday language.

As a consultant or in the role of project leader, I have been involved in successful implementations, some achieving Class "A" certification status. I believe education and training of individuals from top management to end-user contributed greatly to the success of these projects.

I first earned my CIERP certification by passing the CIERP Certification exam in Atlanta, GA. As a consultant and educator, I have found that certification provides credibility, recognizing an individual for their knowledge and capabilities.

For consulting services, training, business meetings, or conference presentations contact:

Ronnie Bishop, CIERP, CPIM, CPM

Author Contact Information:

Email: rbishop48@hotmail.com
Website: www.bishopassociate.com
Phone: 501-414-8629
Address: Bishop & Associates
          P.O. Box 806
          Quincy, Il 62306-0806

▶ Meet Ellen Lucas

Hello, my name is Ellen Lucas. Over the years, I have been involved with many companies who chose to implement ERP within their organizations. One of the first questions that I asked the management staff was to define for me what "ERP" meant to them. This one question usually led into a 'lively' discussion as to the meaning of "ERP". That is why I decided to write this book. I wanted to be able to provide a series of simple, plain answers to commonly asked ERP questions.

I believe that a company's success or failure to implement ERP within their organization begins and ends with understanding the basic concepts of ERP. What is "ERP"? Who 'owns' the ERP system? Is "ERP" an IT project or a business tool that must be managed and maintained? Why do so many ERP implementations fail? Who is responsible for these failures – the project manager, consultant, ERP vendor, or the IT department? Education and training are critical for successfully implementing ERP.

In April 2001, I earned my CIERP certification by passing the CIERP Certification exam in Memphis, TN. Please feel free to contact me at:

Ellen Lucas, CIERP

Author Contact Information:	
Email:	towersecurity@home.com
Website:	www.towersecurity.com
Phone:	219-760-4946
Address:	TowerSecurity, Inc.
	PO Box 15192
	Fort Wayne, IN 46835

Introduction

The purpose of this book is to help people better understand ERP (Enterprise Resource Planning). Through the use of this book people will gain knowledge of what ERP is and is not. This publication is intended for newcomers to ERP or for those looking to establish a basic understanding of this topic.

This book does not represent the end of a journey for those seeking to find the meaning of ERP. Instead it represents the very beginning. We have made every effort to simplify the ERP topic to its most basic level, allowing all people from all areas to gain a better understanding of this challenging and complex subject.

Although we cannot provide you with an ending point for any ERP journey, we do provide a solid foundation in which to begin your journey and "tracks" for you to follow in finding answers to your specific questions. We have simplified the process of learning by providing the starting questions that any new student should be asking. For each question we provide an answer, often more than one. The layout of the book is arranged in question / answer format. As a reader you play the role of a student, an executive, an employee, or other, asking questions. The authors of the book provide the corresponding answer as if you, the reader, are the person asking the question. All questions and answers are part of the online wizard.

The online wizard tool, www.cibres.com/wizard, that accompanies this book, is a unique tool that allows individuals to greatly expand their knowledge seeking options that could not otherwise be done with this publication alone. Students can search for specific questions, or answers, and then drill down into the topic for additional information and web links. The amount of information contained in the online tool is much more comprehensive than that contained in this publication. However, we encourage the newcomer to first review this publication before using the online tool. This will help the early student establish a stronger foundation for understanding the topic of ERP.

All of us at the CIBRES organization wish you the very best in use of the publication and the online wizard tool. We hope that your ERP journey will be completed successfully.

Icons Used In This Book...

Icon	Description
Cibres	Information about the Cibres organization or related products and services.
Sly	Beware of consultants & software, etc.
Warning	Warning, use caution!
Ignorance	Top management sometimes wants to be unaware
Key	Key to creating success in ERP.

Icon	Description
Beware	Beware! Easy to get in trouble.
Reading	Reading materials
Investigate	Investigate
Remember	Remember

Contents

1. What is ERP?   1

2. How can this help my company?   37

3. What's it going to take?   73

4. Who is going to do it?   109

5. How is it going to happen?   131

6. How do we measure success?   173

1

ERP is a software tool used by many companies as a way to run their business. ERP is an evolutionary product that had its origins in the 1950s, the period when people first started to apply computers to business applications. However, with 4 decades of development we find that it is still far from reaching its final evolutionary form. ERP vendors are constantly coming out with aggressive technologies that promise to out leap the competition. Despite these great advances in ERP technology, most companies fail in their attempts to implement and use ERP systems. Companies are forced to use these failing systems to prevent themselves from using traditional paper based systems.

In this chapter the reader will learn...

1. What is ERP?
2. What is ERM?
3. How is ERP used in business?
4. What roles do people play?
5. What are some common misconceptions?

Question:	What is this thing called ERP?

Ellen: ERP is the acronym for Enterprise Resource Planning. It is an integrated software solution that allows everyone within a business organization enterprise to exchange information with each other by accessing a centralized database. ERP helps to 'tear' down the traditional walls between finance, sales, production, and distribution by integrating all facets of a business into a single source of information for managing the business.

Cibres
More information is available in the book ERP: A-Z Implementer's Guide for Success. CIBRES item number 4516.

Ronnie: Exactly, Ellen, and I'd like to add that ERP is an outgrowth of MRPII systems and uses new technology to provide a complete enterprise software solution designed to support and automate business processes. ERP software provides the ability to integrate and share information companywide. ERP software consists of modules, with each module representing a function of the enterprise.

Some examples of functional modules are accounts receivable, accounts payable, general ledger, quality assurance, order entry, human resources, information services, production and inventory control, purchasing, distribution, warehousing, engineering, product development, and facility management. Other modules are available, depending on the structure and the needs of the company and the software vendor. Each function within the organization is represented in the modules, and integration of the modules is stressed to reduce duplication of data entry.

Question: How do I know that ERP is not another passing fad? First it was MRP, then MRP II, and now they are calling it ERP. What's next, ERP II?

Ellen: I understand your frustration. It is true that ERP evolved from MRP – Material Requirements Planning. It is important to remember that while terminology to describe these informational systems may change, organizational needs for accessing the information to operate their business have not changed. ERP systems do not represent a 'new' concept in manufacturing or Information Technology (IT) management, but rather is simply the next phase of a constantly evolving technological market. Over the past 30 years, these systems have continued to help keep businesses functioning.

Prior to 1960, companies were primarily dependent upon paper-produced reports to run their manufacturing operations. The ability to access information depended upon how quickly and accurately these paper reports could be compiled. By the time management received the information, much of it was already outdated.

In the mid-60's, computers arrived on the scene. The computer provided companies with a means to integrate business information that had previously been maintained manually. As companies became familiar with the new technology, they recognized the benefits of being able to not only generate MRP reports but also to integrate other data into the system – making it an effective tool for planning all the resources in the manufacturing environment. MRPII evolved directly from MRP.

In the early 1990's, ERP systems emerged. Many organizations could not understand why they needed a 'new' system when there were no perceptive differences between MRPII and ERP systems. Both systems addressed the same manufacturing information concepts. What was not clearly recognizable at the time was that the main difference between the 2 systems was technical in nature. The software architecture was very different. ERP systems were designed with graphical user interfaces (GUI), client/server architecture, and were not limited to a proprietary operating platform, such as AS400, IBM390, or VAX. ERP systems were able to address technological as well as business functional barriers that MRP and MRPII could not.

As computer technology advances and improves, the information systems needed by companies to run their businesses will continue to evolve. One example of this is the Internet and the necessity for some companies to do business with their customers and vendors via the Internet.

Ronnie: Let me add that ERP is NOT the end all. However, it should not be classified as new or as a passing fad. Industry analysts predict that every major manufacturing company will purchase some type of ERP software package. As technological advances continue, improved capabilities of software will continue. Just as MRPII was an improvement of MRP, ERP is an improvement of MRPII. The next logical step from ERP is ERM, Enterprise Resource Management. However, to take the step to ERM, ERP must first be in place to provide the tools for management. Customer

Relationship Management (CRM), Supply Chain Management (SCM), and Electronic Commerce applications are already being incorporated into some ERP packages and the trend to do so will continue to increase.

Just as the term BRP (Business Resource Planning) is no longer used, the term ERP may change at some point in the future. The term may change, but the concepts will not change. As technology changes, so will the software packages. But the concepts utilized in ERP software packages and the use of ERP by business enterprises to assist in the management of the business will not change.

Question: Could you suggest some good websites to visit to learn the basics of ERP?

Ellen: One of the best ERP websites to visit is maintained by the CIBRES Organization (www.cibres.com). Besides ERP educational material and training, you can find links to other websites, a host of magazine articles, and other ERP resources. You can also take a sample test to see if you have the 'right' stuff to become CIERP-certified. You can also chat online with other ERP professionals.

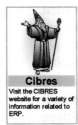

Cibres
Visit the CIBRES website for a variety of information related to ERP.

Another good website to visit is the ERP Fan Club and User Forum (www.erpfans.com). At this site you can exchange ideas and answers to ERP questions with other ERP professionals from around the world, find books and articles on ERP, become up-to-date on current ERP news, and search for jobs in ERP. No membership or registration is required to join the website. It also has links to other websites dealing with specific software solutions, such as Baan, JD Edwards, Oracle, Peoplesoft, and SAP.

ITtoolbox ERP (www.erpassist.com) is another website you may want to check out. It contains links to various resources, such as consulting firms, organizations, ERP recruiters, and software training. Discussion groups for a variety of ERP solutions are maintained. Here you can find solutions to problems by exchanging ideas with other ERP professionals. You can also access a wide variety of written materials such as books, documents, press releases, ERP news, ERP stock reports, and an event calendar. A job bank is also available to you on this site.

Visit www.techrepublic.com to find information and articles on ERP and CRM. TechRepublic offers a variety of weekly newsletters that contain tips, tricks, and the latest ERP-CRM news for the ERP enthusiast. You can pick and choose which newsletters you want to subscribe to. These are free – at no cost to you. Besides ERP and CRM information, the TechRepublic website has information pertaining to other technology subjects, such as operating systems, disaster recovery, etc.

Ronnie: I agree, Ellen. For a site where you can learn the basics of ERP, I recommend the CIBRES website as a starting place. The CIBRES site provides information regarding ERP educational materials, educational seminars, and ERP related articles online. The site also provides an online question wizard that allows for online question and answer sessions.

Other sites you may find beneficial to visit are www.cio.com, www.erpassist.com (ITtoolbox ERP), www.erpsupersuite.com, and www.compinfo-center.com. Each of these sites offer ERP related news and articles. www.APICS.org is the home site for APICS which also offers offers a wealth of educational materials. www.BizDegree.com may prove helpful for business students as a resource for educational assistance.

Question: What are some of the major functions of an ERP system?

Ronnie: The functions of an ERP system are the commonly understood functions of a normal business process. Some of the major functions of an ERP system are payroll, purchasing, accounts receivable and accounts payable, general ledger, inventory control, human resources, product design, order entry, materials planning, production planning, master scheduling, quality assurance, maintenance, and warehousing.

The functions of the ERP system should reflect the functions performed by the business. Not all businesses perform the same functions. For example, a retail business would not use a production schedule whereas a production schedule would be essential for a manufacturing company.

Ellen: Yes, Ronnie, and as you know ERP systems are modular in design. The software core functional modules are divided into suites with each suite addressing specific business activities such as finance, production, and distribution. Additional modules may be added to the core system. For example, a business may need a 'powerful' sales module to help them maintain sales leads, salesman data, sales statistical data, etc. This usually requires an SFA (Sales Force Automation) module where all sales and marketing information can be maintained, updated quickly, and analyzed.

Let's examine some of the business functions addressed within the core suites of an ERP solution. The functional modules that may be found within the Accounting Suite are Address Book, Accounts Receivable, Accounts Payable, General Ledger, Budgeting, Cash Flows, Financial and P&L.

The Manufacturing Suite usually contains functions to manage items, bills of material, routings, work centers, group technology and documents such as CAD drawings. Purchasing, Inventory Control, Quality Assurance, Job Orders, Finite Scheduling, and Shop Floor Control are functions found within the manufacturing suite of most ERP solutions.

The Distribution Suite usually contains Order Processing, Quotations, Customer Profiling, Item Profiling, Marketing and Sales, Pricing, Freight and Carrier data, Warehouse Management, Shipping and Receiving, EDI and multiple reports.

These are only a few of the functions that are associated with ERP. There are others which may be added, such as CRM, that can assist companies to run their businesses more efficiently.

Question: Computers have been around for 50 years; why all the excitement over ERP now?

Ronnie: Even though computers have been around for 50 years, a look at the history of ERP will explain why there is so much excitement and emphasis on ERP now. In the mid 50's the APICS organization was founded as an educational society for production and inventory control practitioners. Through the use of "new" computer techniques, new methods for controlling inventory were developed. From then through the 60's, the focus of software, used by manufacturers, was placed on inventory control. Software packages for the most part were designed utilizing traditional inventory concepts and most packages were usually customized.

With increased computerized capabilities in late 60's and into the 70's, Material Requirements Planning (MRP) systems became the focus of industry. MRP was based on the concept of translating a demand into a Master Schedule for end items, and time-phasing the net requirements for the components, sub-assemblies, and raw materials. This provided a plan for the purchasing and production of materials.

The concept of MRP was expanded into MRP II (Manufacturing Resource Planning) in the 80's.

With increased capabililties and integration, production or shop floor activities and distribution activities could be planned and managed more effectively. During the 80's it was also recognized that these concepts could and should be utilized by all business enterprises, not just manufacturing companies.

MRPII was an improvement from MRP, but it did not satisfy the needs of the total business enterprise. In the 90's, MRPII was expanded to include functional areas such as Human Resources, Accounting, Project Management, Facilities Management, Product Design, Engineering, etc. The functions of the entire business enterprise were now covered, thus the term, ERP (Enterprise Resource Planning).

In addition to the aforementioned history of ERP, the advances in computer technology made computers more accessible than they were 50 years ago. 50 years ago, computers were large and very expensive to use. Computers processed information faster than humans, but were still very slow when compared to today's speed. In the 50's, the use of home computers was unforeseen. In the 60's and 70's, major companies had computer capabilities, but only for select applications. CRT "dumb terminals" were made available for data entry and processing. In the 80's and 90's, companies began replacing CRT's with desktop computers. With advanced technology, such as computer chips, the cost of personal computers decreased dramatically. Processing speeds and data storage capabilities increased. Now, laptops and portable hand held units have more memory and are less expensive than desktops were then. As processing capabilities increase and relative costs decrease, ERP applications will continue to increase.

Ellen: Yes, Ronnie; computers have been around for 50 years, but as you so aptly stated, technology has not always been as innovative as it is today. The computer technology has been in a constant state of change. It has gradually improved in speed, capability, and flexibility. As computer technology advanced, companies looked for ways to use this technology in their business environment.

ERP has become the tool by which companies can harness the power of computer technology and blend it with business processes. Many ERP solutions have given companies the ability to reach out via the Internet to customers, vendors, and other facilities.

Question: What are some key components that make up an ERP system? What must a software system have to qualify as an ERP system?

Ellen: There are 3 key elements that every ERP software system must have:

Remember
The three things that make up an ERP system include function, integration, and data. All three must work with the people that use an ERP system.

Functionality: An ERP system is made up of modules. Each of those modules can be 'tied' to specific business process flows or functions that define how a business is run. For example, the payroll function must be done for a company to stay in business. Other common functions may include accounts payable, accounts receivable, general ledger, purchasing, sales quotes, sales orders, MRP, production-shop floor control, job costing, forecasting, scheduling, shipping, etc. It is not unusual for ERP systems to have 100 or more of these business functions.

Integration: Integration between the modules within an ERP system provides for connectivity between the functional process flows. You can also think of 'integration' as a method for communicating data between the business process flows. This communication allows data to be entered once and shared between the functional modules within the ERP system. The method by which this 'communication' takes place is largely dependent upon technology. Source code, databases, local area networks, Internet, email, wide area networks, and protocols are some of the common ways in which communication takes place through the integration in an ERP system.

Data: Data is information specific to a company. Customer, vendor, and item information are examples of the type of data that is stored within master database files of the ERP system.

Ronnie: Yes, Ellen, I agree that funtionality, integration, and data are 3 elements that every ERP system must have, but I'd say that probably most important of all the key elements of an ERP system is people. People can and have performed all the tasks that software performs. Some businesses still operate manual systems with all the functionality of computer based systems.

Whether the system is a computer based software package or a manual human system, it must have integration to qualify as an ERP system. Integration of functional areas for sharing common data is a must for any ERP system.

Question: So tell me a little about yourself. How did you become involved in ERP and CIBRES?

Ellen: I have been involved with ERP for approximately 20 years. My degree is in computer programming. My career in ERP began when I 'interned' at a small metal fabrication shop in Logansport, IN. They asked me to write a program that would help them track their orders, fill the orders, ship the orders, and invoice the customer. The company used my program for 3 years until it was decided that the company needed an integrated solution.

My experience with ERP covers system selections, implementations, trainer and educator, support, maintenance, etc. Besides having a good working knowledge and experience in ERP, I also know the accounting and operation side of the business, since my last position was as a controller and system administrator.

In 1996, I founded TowerSecurity, Inc. It was my goal to provide other companies with ERP consulting services at a fair price. In the early spring of 2001, I was doing research on the Internet and came across the CIBRES website. I noted that they were offering an ERP certification seminar and exam to be held in Memphis, TN in April, 2001. I contacted the organization to obtain information regarding the certification and after speaking with them I decided to attend the seminar. Upon further investigation, I decided to require everyone at TowerSecurity, Inc. to take the exam and become certified. I felt that the certification was extremely important. It would be a means of demonstrating to clients that we know ERP and have the skills necessary to assist them.

I'm proud to be part of a small but growing number of professional people who can use the CIERP – certified notation after their name.

Ronnie:　For more than 30 years, I have been involved in manufacturing and distribution either as a consultant, an educator, or as a company employee. I founded Bishop & Associates to provide management consulting and educational services for businesses and industry. I have held the positions of Division Director of Materials Management, Materials Manager, Accounting Manager, and Quality Assurance Manager. As Project Leader, I have implemented ERP, MRPII, MRP, and ISO/QS systems, obtaining class A certification and ISO/QS registration. As an educator, I conduct ERP certification seminars, I have taught college classes for more than 10 years, and I teach APICS certification review classes.

My involvement in ERP was a natural outgrowth of my involvement in MRPII and ISO/QS implementations. As a consultant and educator, I continually strive to stay aware of the best business practices and tools available for successfully managing a business of any type.

One day while searching the web for information about ERP, I clicked into www.cibres.com, and thus began my involvement in CIBRES. At the time, there were not many websites or organizations offering information about ERP. CIBRES was and still is the only organization offering certification for implementors of ERP systems (CIERP). Having been a member of APICS and certified (CPIM) for 20 years, I recognize the benefits of education and certification for both employees and employers. I was impressed with the CIBRES ERP educational materials. I attended one of the CIBRES certification seminars, passed the CIERP examination, and became an associate.

Question: What exactly is CIBRES?

Ronnie: CIBRES is an acronym for Communicating Integrated Business Resource Enterprise Solutions. CIBRES is a world wide organization consisting of educators, practitioners, business leaders, and students working together to bring about business excellence through the use of research, education, and communication of management and communication technology.

The CIBRES website, www.cibres.com, provides ERP related articles, ERP educational materials, and an online wizard that allows individuals to have their ERP related questions answered by Certified ERP practitioners. CIBRES is the only organization that offers certification in ERP.

CIBRES is currently developing a new certification for e-business professionals, CIEB standing for Certified Implementer of E-business. This certification program will begin in early 2002. Individuals that achieve the CIEB will have demonstrated they have the knowledge and understanding to make e-business successful. Also, a higher level certification, CMEB standing for Certified Master of E-business will be offered in 2002. To obtain this level of certification, an individual must complete both the CIERP and CIEB certifications plus additional requirements.

Ellen:

Cibres

"ERP: A-Z Implementer's Guide for Success" is the #1 selling book on ERP around the world in over 50 different countries. Individuals can read chapter one online from the CIBRES website (www.cibres.com) and read reviews. CIBRES item number 4516.

Yes, Ronnie; CIBRES was founded by Mr. Travis Anderegg, a leading authority on ERP. The organization works with business leaders, educators, and students to provide a wide variety of educational, training, and technical resources to individuals who are involved with ERP.

You can see the dedication of this organization to promote the advancement of business through education by visiting their website. You can access ERP articles containing information written by CIERP (Certified Implementer of Enterprise Resource Planning) certified individuals. You can order educational materials online, such as the publication, ***ERP: A-Z Implementer's Guide for Success***. You can see if you have the right 'stuff' to pass the CIERP examination by taking a sample test online. CIERP certification seminar and exam locations are listed in case you want to become CIERP-certified and join the ranks of a small but growing group of professionals who have achieved this title. The site also has a chat forum where you can exchange information and ask questions of other ERP professionals. Links to other ERP websites and sources of information are also listed for you to access.

Question: What is the difference between ERP and ERM?

Ellen:

Cibres

ERM came from the CIBRES organization. CIBRES coined the term to help companies better understand problems with their ERP systems.

ERP is simply a software tool that a company can use to help run the business. As I previously stated, the ERP system is made up of 3 fundamental key elements: functionality, integration, and data. For companies to successfully integrate an ERP system with their daily operational activities requires much more than simply implementing the ERP system. It requires that companies integrate and synchronize their business functions using ERM – Enterprise Resource Management.

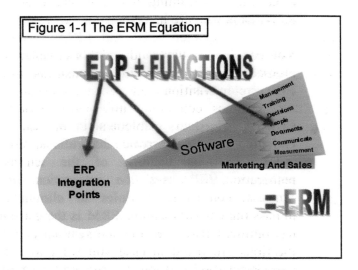

Figure 1-1 The ERM Equation

The ERM formula can be stated as: ERP (Integration + Functional Software Modules) + Business Functions = ERM

The business functions in the ERM formula refer to people, processes, and resources that exist outside of the ERP software system. This would include management, training, decisions, people, documents, communication, performance measurements, marketing, and sales.

ERM – Enterprise Resource Management – includes certain characteristics of ERP but the emphasis is on 'resource' and 'management'. ERM is the tools and techniques needed to manage the resources within an enterprise. ERP is simply one of those resources that needs to be managed.

It is important that companies understand the difference between ERP and ERM. Companies that do not understand this difference often experience difficulties before, during, and after an ERP implementation.

Ronnie: ERP is the business software solution used for the entire business enterprise that allows for the planning and utilization of the enterprise's resources. ERP uses the integration of the functional software modules to eliminate the duplication of information. ERM is the combining of the functionality of the software with each of the functions of the business and is a tool to aid in utilizing the information to "manage" the business enterprise.

So, in a nutshell, ERP should be thought of as the complete business enterprise wide software solution while ERM is ERP plus the functional activities that occur within each module and business process.

Question: What are some common misconceptions regarding ERP?

Ellen: Misconception #1: This 'new' ERP system will correct any and all problems that a company may be experiencing.

An ERP system is nothing more than a business tool. Its success or failure lies with the people who maintain it. It is not a 'cure all' for problems that a company may be experiencing. For example, a company I worked with had implemented 3 different ERP systems within 5 years. They said that each one of these did not meet their needs and they could not get accurate, financial data from the system. When I spoke with the sales and purchasing departments I found that none of the people even used the data coming from the system because as they said, "It's not correct. We can't trust the numbers." After evaluating the system and the internal processes, I found that there was nothing wrong with the ERP solution. The company was only utilizing about 25% of the entire system, no procedures or controls were being followed within the company, no one had taken 'ownership' of the system and management looked upon the system as an IT project.

In this case, the most expensive, biggest, and best ERP system would not have solved the company problems. The company had to address internal issues, establish controls and procedures for the system and supporting functions, and correct the inaccurate data that had already been entered into the system.

Misconception #2: Joe Smith uses a particular ERP system. He says it works well for his company. He does the same thing that we do. Let's skip the selection process and just implement the same ERP system that he has.

Why is this thinking wrong? Mr. Smith's business plan may be vastly different from your company. You may have overseas locations or multi-lingual issues; he may not. You may have a totally different organizational structure than he, which a system must address. Your business processes and the manner in which you do business can be different.

The best method for choosing an ERP solution is by establishing an ERP system selection process. This will help you make the best choice because it will be based on *your* business critical criteria and processes, not someone else's.

Misconception #3: The ERP vendor can tell us what we need. They know and understand ERP.

The ERP vendor knows his/her product. In some cases, an ERP vendor does not know the basic concepts of ERP. Most importantly, the ERP vendor does not know *your* business, how *your* business functions and what the future business plans for *your* company are. A company who leaves their ERP decision to a vendor will usually be disappointed with the outcome of the project.

Ronnie: I agree, Ellen; the #1 misconception that companies have regarding ERP is that ERP systems are a cure all, that they will remove all the problems the business may have. An ERP system is only software that will provide the tools necessary for improvement. However, the software must be properly implemented, users trained, and the information obtained (from using the software) must be used. In many instances, companies implement the software, but do not achieve the results expected because users at some or all levels of the organization do not know how to use the software or information obtained from the software.

Another common misconception is that with the implementation of an ERP sytem, a business will gain customers and/or sales will increase. Implementation of the system alone does not guarantee an increase in customers or sales. This can be a benefit as a result of using the software to improve the business operation and improve customer service.

Many companies believe the bigger the system, the better the system. That is a very common and, in most cases, costly misconception. The size of the system is relative to the size and needs of the company. Some companies purchase large, complicated systems that contain functional modules that are not needed by the company. The cost of the software and the cost of implementation is greater than would be required for a smaller system that would fill the company's requirements.

Another especially common misconception is that ERP vendors understand the basic fundamental concepts of ERP. It is understandable to expect the vendors to know and understand ERP concepts, but that is not always the case. The vendor is just selling a software product and does not necessarily understand the use, the concepts, or the value of ERP.

Early in my career, I was produce manager in a grocery store in a small southern town. I was a very good manager. I knew how to merchandise the product, how much and what to order, and was a good salesperson. But, I am not much of a cook. One day a customer asked me how to prepare a "new" vegetable we had received, and I proceeded to explain how to peel, boil, and season, this vegetable. Well, to say the least, it was not a very appetizing dish when she had finished preparing it. I had made a sale but had a very unhappy customer. Why? Because I did not know what I should have known about the product. That is the same with many ERP vendors.

Question: What is the average life expectancy of an ERP system?

Ellen: The average life expectancy of an ERP system is 15 years. It is considered a 'best practice' recommendation that a company perform an evaluation of their ERP system as well as their current business processes every 5 to 7 years. Company organizational structure, strategic business plans, company vision, and technology requirements can change over time rendering the once full-featured ERP system outdated.

Ronnie: There are several different views on the expected life of an ERP system. Most commonly, as Ellen stated, the life expectancy of a new implementation is 10 to 15 years, but with technologies advancing so rapidly 7-10 years may be more accurate now. However, that does not mean that the total system is completely outdated. I'd say an evaluation of the system should be done every 3-5 years. Just as with other aspects of our lives, technology is constantly changing. Technological advances are happening at such a rapid rate that even personal computers are outdated almost by the time you can purchase one and get it installed.

Software development progresses with much greater speed than ever before due to the programming tools available now.

Remember that ERP is not just computers and software, but people, processes, and functions. It's easy to understand why the life expectancy of any system is very short. Quality systems and standards are forever changing. Customer expectations and demands change daily. Business needs change constantly. So, it is necessary for ERP systems to change rapidly also.

Question: I heard several sources say that ERP is nothing more than our people system. What do they mean by that?

Ronnie: I have made that statement myself. An ERP system is based on a manual system for doing things. Before computers became so widely utilized for storing and processing data, people performed these functions. Now with computerization so prevalent, an ERP system is no better than the people using the software. Too often, ERP software is installed with little consideration given to the people that will be using the software. The end users must be educated and trained. If the end users do not know the capabilities of the software, the software will not be a useful tool for them.

Remember

People are important for the successful use and implementation of an ERP system.

Successful implementation and use of any system, manual or computerized, is dependant upon people. Computer software is only a tool for the people to use to perform tasks more efficiently. Any business enterprise must have functions and process flows that are efficient and effective to be successful, and these functions and processes are only as good as the people performing them.

Accurate data is essential for the successful performance of an ERP system. People are responsible for the accuracy of this data. Decisions that affect the business are made based on the data, decisions that are made by people. An ERP system is no better than the people implementing, maintaining, and using it.

Ellen: Yes Ronnie, as you know, for many years, companies   conducted   business   without   a computer. Information was collected and maintained on paper by people within the company. The accuracy of this information was dependent upon the people who maintained it. This still applies today.

ERP is a complete enterprise wide software solution. It is a business tool designed to help companies operate their businesses in an efficient, productive manner. As with any tool, it must be managed and maintained. That requires human intervention – people.

Users of the system are people who enter, maintain, and analyze the data that builds the databases of information contained within the system. Customer, vendor, and item master files are examples of the types of databases that serve as 'cornerstones' of an ERP system.

Business processes and procedures are needed to make sure that the data being entered into the system is accurate and complete. The ERP software solution has internal code that directs the flow of information within the software modules, but external processes and procedures must be defined by management (people) within a company. The blending of external processes and procedures with the ERP solution is dependent upon people.

People are key to a successful ERP project. ERP is a people system. Many ERP projects have either failed to be implemented, failed shortly after implementation, or suffered data corruption because of the lack of people involvement and commitment.

Question: What is the difference between an ERP vendor and an ERP service provider?

Ellen: An ERP vendor sells and services a particular ERP solution. Made2Manage, SAP, Oracle, and JD Edwards are examples of these various packaged ERP solutions. ERP vendors own and maintain the source code needed to run the ERP application. They provide software upgrades, customer technical support, training, and a variety of other services that are needed by end users of their ERP solution.

While the ERP vendor sells the ERP solution, an ERP service provider can provide companies the needed resources to support the ERP solution itself. These resources may be in the form of services such as business application services, IT technical support services, project management services, and outsourcing services. The ERP service provider can also furnish products needed to support the ERP solution, such as equipment and software.

Ronnie: And let me add, Ellen, that an ERP vendor may also be a service provider, but not *all* vendors *are* service providers. The ERP vendor owns the source code for the ERP software programs and periodically provides upgrades to the software.

ERP service providers focus mainly on providing ERP related services and products. These services may include technical consulting, application consulting, business management consulting, and project management.

Question: How does ERP work for a retail store?

Ellen: The retail market is a relatively late-bloomer when it comes to ERP. This is in part due to the fact that the retail market is a unique type of industry. This uniqueness involves types of items that are marketed, the complexity of the retail business processes, and the need to be competitive in pricing and service.

Retailers need ERP solutions to help them create, manage, fulfill, and analyze customers' demands. There are 4 major business processes that are vital to a retail operation: (1) CRM – Customer Relation Management; (2) SCM – Supply Chain Management; (3) Logistics – Distribution; (4) Merchandise – Marketing.

An example of a retail market that is highly visible to consumers is the grocery store. One major grocery chain recognized that if they wanted to stay competitive they had to update their technology systems. Most of the company's applications were custom written and had not been updated for several years. These custom written applications were not integrated. The ability to analyze any of the data in these applications was not available. The grocery retailer suffered from vast information gaps since their 'home-grown' systems often lacked clear information as to what was being sold in the stores. Once an item was sent to the store, visibility of that product was lost. The ability to track perishable products was critical. Perishable items have different shelf lives and demand different types of warehousing. With dairy products, it's important to maintain a "cold chain" throughout the product's life from purchasing, warehousing, and distribution. Purchasing becomes more complicated in the grocery market because items are purchased locally, regionally, nationally, or internationally.

An integrated ERP solution for the retail grocery market holds all item and merchandising information into a common core system. Functionality within the ERP solution would include category management, merchandising, procurement, promotion, pricing, and forecasting – including the perishable side of the business. Besides the core retail applications for purchasing, merchandising and inventory management, the system would also integrate with the financial, human resource, warehouse management, and logistics aspects of the business. A web-enabled supply chain, SCM, enables the retailer to improve relations with their vendors and customers. Information from customer purchases can be analyzed; thus, giving the retailer the opportunity to provide better customer service. Products can be monitored both at the POS – point of sale – and for shelf-life; thereby, allowing shelves to be stocked with the most desired and freshest products. Self-checkout lines allow customers to scan the items and pay online; thus eliminating long lines at the traditional checkout cash registers.

In summary, an ERP solution designed for the retail environment aids retailers to cut their management costs, improve customer service, track products through the system, maintain inventory levels, and perform analysis on the data collected from customer sales and inquiries.

Ronnie: Application of ERP in a retail store is designed to: assist the retailer in improving customer service, maintain adequate inventory levels, collect sales data, and reduce costs. These are basically the same functions desired from other environments that utilize ERP. However, as Ellen stated, the retail market is one of the new frontiers for ERP applications. The retail markets are realizing they too can benefit from the same basic information structures that manufacturing enterprises use, even though they differ greatly.

In a retail store environment, the integrated ERP solution would provide the common functionality of purchasing, inventory management, and financial applications. Depending on the size of the enterprise, other functional aspects that retailers might require include forecasting, logistics, and human resources. Point of sale data collection may also be desired.

Ellen, as you may know, I've had the opportunity to tour one of the nation's largest retailers and do a "walk through" to witness how their system works. I visited their headquarters, several distribution locations, and stores and observed the following steps:

1. Item information is collected at point of sale by scanning for price at retail location.
2. Scanned price and item information is fed back into the database.
3. The database tracks sales of that product at that particular location.
4. Replenishment request is automatically generated when sales reach a particular level.
5. Replenishment request is transmitted to the distribution center that services the retail location.
6. An order is generated that includes the stocking location for that product.
7. Product sales data is collected and analyzed to provide the best mix of product and the most appropriate stocking levels for that product by geographical area.

Question: How does ERP work for a process environment, such as the oil refinery?

Ellen: It is very important that process manufacturers (such as an oil refinery) implement an ERP solution that is designed to address the special needs of a process environment. Many ERP vendors have tried to blend the requirements into a solution that addresses both manufacturing requirements; but as companies try to implement these solutions, they usually experience much difficulty.

The primary differences between a discrete manufacturer and a process manufacturer are directly linked to the inventory and production modules of the ERP solution. These modules deal with the processing and usage of materials that are needed to meet and satisfy customer demands. Solids, powder, liquid, gas, wire, and plastic pellets are a few of the types of raw materials often used in a processing plant. Each of these materials possesses their own basic characteristics. These characteristics often define the length of the material's shelf-life. They may be purchased in one unit of measure, inventoried in another unit of measure, and used in a recipe at another unit of measure.

In a process environment the raw materials and production processes needed to produce the end product (such as oil or gas) are modeled into a 'recipe'. The 'recipe' can be simple or complex – depending upon the end product.

In a typical process-manufacturing situation, material defined in the 'recipe' is assembled to process an order. A quality control technician will test the material to make sure that it meets a range of acceptable specifications. The test results are recorded. During the processing of the material, the expected yield of the process may be less or more than expected. In fact, the actual quantity and quality of the finished product will vary each time production is 'run'. The finished product is again tested by a quality control technician. The results (which often vary) are recorded.

A process ERP solution must be designed to handle all of the various factors that are associated with the process-manufacturing environment. Purchasing, managing and storage of inventory, production, by-products, co-products, recycling of material, waste, production variations, production yield losses and gains are some of the unique features that any process ERP solution needs to address.

Ronnie: The design of the ERP solution for a process environment includes methods for addressing special needs associated with the particular processes. Oil fineries present challenges that do not exist in most manufacturing environments. Some unique features that might exist for process environment applications include:

- Byproducts,
- Recycled material,
- Classification,
- Inventory storage, and
- Variability of recipes or mixtures.

Inventory management and production scheduling for process manufacturing usually differ greatly from discrete manufacturing methods.

In process manufacturing environments there is normally a larger degree of variation in production quality and quantity, from one batch or run to the next, than exists in discrete manufacturing. Monitoring the quality of the product and the yeild / loss of product is required more often.

Question: How does ERP work for a manufacturing environment?

Ellen: There are many ERP solutions on the market that meet the needs of the manufacturing environment. These solutions can range from SME (small-mid size systems) to SAP or Oracle (very large systems). Which system a company chooses depends upon their:

- Strategic business plan,
- Current and future organizational structure,
- Current and future business process needs,
- Future technology plans, and
- Future business plans.

Customer information is updated in the ERP system. A sales quote is generated in the sales module and sent to the customer. If the customer accepts the quote and issues an order, a sales order is generated in the system. In many ERP systems, a sales order can be generated automatically from the sales quote that was issued previously. As soon as the sales order is generated, the ERP system automatically looks at the ship date on the order. The system then checks inventory levels to ascertain whether the order can be filled from existing finished product. If the order can be filled with existing inventory, the system flags the inventory and allocates it for that particular order. If there is insufficient inventory, the system will either automatically generate a job order for the needed material or notify production that material is needed to fill the order. Upon confirmation of a job order, the system compares the BOM – Bills of material – with inventory levels to make sure that the materials needed to produce and fill the order are available. If the inventory is not sufficient, the system notifies the purchasing department that the material needs to be purchased from the vendor. Purchasing orders the required material from the vendor. The purchased material is received and allocated to that job. Now that all the raw material is available, the job order needs to be scheduled for production. The product router is checked to see what production steps, equipment, and work centers are required to produce the product. The job is then scheduled and released for production. The product is produced; quality control checks the product for compliance and records results; product is packaged and shipped to customer. The accounting department bills the customer, collects the customer's payment, processes the invoice for the material that was ordered from the vendor, and issues a payment to the vendor.

This scenario is typically what happens in a discrete manufacturing environment. Of course, there are other support activities, such as customer service, checking the status of the customer's order, and accounting, are performed during the production cycle. A discrete manufacturer gets few surprises during this cycle if the BOM and routers are accurate and updated as needed. Inventory accuracy is also essential for the purchasing and MRP to be reliable.

Ronnie: ERP evolved from MRPII, which evolved from MRP, which was primarily designed to assist manufacturing in controlling inventory. However, now ERP software is designed to work for any type of organization through integration of functional modules. Manufacturing companies represent the largest number of users and utilize more modules than most other businesses.

ERP systems for manufacturing environments normally allow for tracking customer information, financial results, inventory and production management, warehousing, human resources, maintainance, asset management, and quality assurance. Sales/customer orders can be tracked from beginning to end. Purchase orders may be tracked from request for quote, to placing the order, to receipt of product. Shop floor or production orders can be monitored throughout the production process. Deliveries to the customers can be tracked from receipt of order, to manufacture of product, to shipment of product, to receipt of product by the customer. Inventory levels can be planned and monitored. Shop capacity, human resource requirements, quality assurance applications, and facilities maintenance can be tracked in the system.

A typical example of how the ERP system functions and the information that's provided could relate to a customer order. Using ERP modules, the customer order can be traced from the time the order is received until the customer receives the order. The order is input into the system, which creates a demand for inventory to satisfy the order requirements. The MRP module compares the on hand inventory balance against the demand which could result in a requirement to produce more inventory of the product. A shop order is created to produce more of the product, utilizing the bill of material, routing, and inventory information; a demand may be placed to purchase more raw materials required to produce the product. The date the customer requested the product dictates the date the raw material is needed so production of the product on the shop floor can be completed in time for shipment to the customer. Schedules for production and shipment are derived from the customer request date. The product is shipped to the customer based on customer, carrier, and freight information which exists in the database. But that is not the end of the process. Accounting uses the shop hours required to produce the product plus the materials used to accumulate a cost for the product. These actual costs are compared to predetermined standard costs to evaluate whether manufacturing and selling that product was profitable. Other factors are also included in the process and other information is utilized, but this is a thumbnail picture of the process.

2

How can this help my company?

Most companies fail to use ERP successfully. Does this mean that companies should stop using ERP? No, even a failing system is more beneficial than no system at all. There is no replacement for an ERP system. As long as we have businesses, data, and data processing needs we will have ERP systems. ERP provides great opportunities to streamline business process flows, allowing organizations the opportunity to provide faster service and better products. A well designed and implemented ERP system acts as an organization's digital nervous system. It allows the organization to reorganize its resources based on customer needs.

In this chapter the reader will learn ...

1. How do I prevent ERP disasters?
2. What are direct benefits of ERP?
3. What is soft coding?
4. How is e-business related to ERP?
5. How does it help companies excel?

Question: I have read about ERP implementations that have turned into nightmares because they had so many problems. How can I make sure that our company has a rapid implementation with few disruptions to our business?

Ellen: Planning, planning, planning – is the key to a successful ERP implementation. You must develop an ERP implementation project plan to be successful. There are no guarantees for success with an ERP implementation. Planning helps you to achieve success.

Investigate
The CIBRES website contains many useful case studies on ERP systems that went wrong.

Gaining senior management involvement and commitment to the ERP project is critical to the success of your ERP implementation. ERP projects require not only monetary resources, but time and people to accomplish the tasks outlined on the implementation project plan. Senior management must let the organization know that they are supporting the project and the project core team.

Follow the project plan by assigning roles and responsibilities to the 'best' people within the organization. Assign dates as to when the assigned task is to be completed. Review the project plan against the completed task. If tasks are not being completed on time, investigate as to the reason why deadlines are being missed; perhaps you underestimated the resources required for the successful completion of the project.

Prepare end users of the system to take 'ownership' of their 'portion' of the system. Many times, this is an area that is overlooked. Keep everyone within the organization informed as to the progress that has been made with the implementation.

Proper planning, senior management commitment, change management, user involvement, and the proper IT infrastructure support are all elements that lead to a successful ERP implementation.

Ronnie:

Beware
ERP projects that lack planning are a disaster waiting to happen.

Many implementations do turn into "nightmares" and I agree with Ellen; planning is the key to a successful implementation. Statistics show the majority of ERP implementations either fail completely or never reach the expected goal. Like any other project, the ERP implementation project is influenced by the company environment or company culture. Most companies are not culturally ready for an ERP implementation. You can do several things to improve the chances for success. You need to examine the reasons for implementing a new system. Management commitment to the project and managing change are key factors in successful implementations.

A good project plan includes a timeline, tasks to be performed, responsibilities for performing tasks, and education and training. These factors will assist in keeping a project moving in the right direction. As Thomas Fuller once said, "A danger foreseen is half avoided." Many of the dangers that might befall or hinder an implementation should be addressed during the project planning meeting, which will establish the vision and mission statements for the project and define the scope of the project.

You need to select a project team with diverse representation of functional areas. The members of the project team should be provided with basic ERP education as well as training of how to use the selected software. The team should have a strong project leader as well as a sponsor from the top management or corporate group. This sponsor, as well as all of top management, must have a strong commitment to the success of the project, and must be able to remove any road blocks that may hinder the progress of the project.

Communication is essential. The communication must be two way, from top management downward and also from end-users upward. Open communication will help relieve some of the fears that always accompany a change. Communication helps to surface potential problems before they become real problems. There must be a compelling reason for the change and this reason must be communicated well. If the reasons for change are not effectively communicated to all involved, the implementation and use of any new system will be hampered.

Question: Why are so very few companies successful with ERP?

Ellen: There are many reasons why few companies successfully implement ERP. Unfortunately, many companies embark on an ERP implementation project without having the education, training, and understanding of ERP concepts.

Key
The key to successful ERP systems is proper education and training. Education must take place prior to purchasing and implementing an ERP system. The CIERP certification program was created for this reason. Visit www.cibres.com for details of the CIERP certification program.

Often, senior management views the ERP solution as just another 'piece' of software. They feel that IT should be able to implement the ERP solution since IT maintains other software. They don't understand the complexity of the ERP implementation; therefore, the senior management does not give top priority to the project.

The amount of time needed to complete the project is underestimated. The amount of time that an implementation will actually require usually exceeds the amount originally anticipated.

Project scope is not clearly defined. The scope of the project directly relates to the number of modules being implemented. It includes all of the functional and technical aspects of the solution that a company wants to implement. Without a clearly defined project scope, ERP implementation can experience 'project scope creep'. This can spell disaster for the success of the ERP implementation.

Underestimating the resources required to implement ERP is another potential 'pitfall' to a successful implementation. Internal people, external consultants, hardware, additional software, technical and application consultants may be limited. All of these resources require money to be allocated to the project. If the company has limited financial funds, this will greatly hamper the success of the implementation.

With every ERP implementation, there are risks. Many times, these risks are not taken into consideration when the ERP project is being considered. Many of these risks are external to the solution being implemented. For example, factors that may pose a risk to the success of an ERP implementation include, user acceptance of the new system, ROI, and documentation.

The complexity of the ERP implementation project is another factor that can contribute to the failure of an ERP project. Every project contains some degree of complexity or difficulty associated with it. Company size, organizational structure, and critical business criteria determine how complex the ERP implementation project may be.

Ronnie: That's correct, Ellen, and as you know 60 to 80 percent of all ERP systems are in trouble. They will be considered either partial failures or complete failures because they never really meet expectations. Why is this? There are several reasons for this high failure rate, including, as you stated, Ellen, lack of support from top management, lengthy implementations, unrealistic expectations, and cost over-runs causing projects to be abandoned.

Too often, top management supports the project initially, but as the project moves forward, the support diminishes. Other problems and projects demand their time, attention, and interest. Many times when this declining support and interest becomes evident to others in the organization, their commitment begins to decline also.

The scope of the project, including expected results, is not always well defined. Many times, the implementation begins without anyone really knowing the expected end results. As the project progresses, participants realize that other areas should be included, that other people should be included, and additional benefits can be realized from expanding the project. This can be an advantage if handled correctly. However, too often, as the project begins to expand, cost over-runs begin occurring because the expanded areas were not included in the additional cost-benefit analysis. Then deadlines begin to be missed because additional resources are not available to do the extra work required to include the additional areas. When this happens, chaos can occur, the project begins to drag, finger pointing begins, and support begins to decrease. The project is abandoned or stopped short of the desired results.

Often, a company considers an implementation a failure because at the project's completion, the problems the business enterprise was experiencing before the implementation still exist. This is not the fault of the software or the implementation team. This is because the business should have performed some "re-engineering" before and during the implementation, but did not. The same old practices produce the same results.

Question: How does a company know when it is time to get a new ERP system? Can many of the problems that we have be fixed without purchasing and installing a new system?

Ronnie: Generally, a company can tell it's time to begin looking for new ERP software when the number of requests for modifications to the existing software become numerous and they request special programming to obtain the needed information. Often times, the costs and time associated with the required programming becomes prohibitive. When the information required to run the business becomes increasingly hard to obtain and drives the need for the additional programming, the company should evaluate the current system.

Also, when a company goes through a business re-engineering project, they may recognize the necessity for a new software package. If a company has not performed business process re-engineering prior to the start of a new implementation, it would be a good idea to perform it during the early stages of the implementation project.

Yes, many of the problems that companies face can be solved without purchasing and installing a new system. You should remember, a new software or system is not a cure-all; it is only a tool to use to run the business. Performing a business process re-engineering helps identify problem areas and allows for solutions to the problems. Sometimes the re-engineering effort may determine a new system is required; other times the result may be just to utilize the currrent system differently. Sometimes all you need are some modifications to the existing software to provide the functionality required. Also, programming changes may be required for gathering data and producing reports. Often these modifications and programming are cost prohibitive.

Many times, all that is required is some additional education and/or training for the employees. Often the real cause of many of the problems a company may face is a lack of understanding of how to effectively use the system. In many implementations, the end users are not properly trained to fully utilize the system. Users are provided with only enough training to perform their job the way someone else has determined the job should be performed. The users are not trained or educated to understand how their tasks relate to other functional areas. With the proper training and education, users can understand how the functions they perform impact other areas.

Ellen: Exactly, Ronnie, companies change and evolve over time. Many times, the company simply outgrows the capability of their current system. For example, a company may start out using a simple system like PeachTree, but over time, management may need costing information that PeachTree cannot provide. The company's vision, business plan, technology plan, organization structure, product and customer requirements are all reasons why a company may want to look at another system.

For example, a process manufacturer might have chosen a system that was designed for a discrete manufacturer. The primary difference is the manner in which their products are inventoried, produced, and sold. A discrete manufacturer deals with 1 bolt and 2 nuts. The process manufacturer deals with ½ pound of flour and 5 cups of sugar. For a process manufacturer to try and use a system not designed for his manufacturing environment is like a person trying to fit a round peg into a square hole.

CIBRES recommends that before a company lay out a large sum of money to purchase another system or upgrade a current system, that the company establish an ERP system selection process. The system selection process will help a company decide whether they need to upgrade the current system, purchase another system, or purchase additional software modules to integrate with their current system.

The system selection process methodology includes such tasks as:

- Looking at a company's current processes,
- Defining critical business functions,
- Defining critical system criteria,
- Evaluating ERP vendors, and
- Looking at possible system solutions, etc.

If a company goes through a system selection process, the decision as to whether to purchase a new system or upgrade the old system will be answered. The system selection process gives a company the facts and basis for making their decision. A company is more apt to choose a system that meets their needs if they perform the system selection process.

Question: Why do many ERP systems run way over budget on implementation costs?

Ellen:

Ignorance
Management all too often is nowhere to be found in an ERP implementation.

With every ERP implementation project, unexpected events can occur that have the potential to send the project into a tailspin. Unexpected management changes, loss of key staff members, or business direction are all reasons why an ERP project may go over budget; however, more often than not, it's the preventable problems that cause the project to go over budget. What are some of these problems?

Problem #1: Lack of Top Management Commitment – Many times, top management doesn't feel that an ERP project is one in which they should devote time or support. They often view it as an IT project, not a business project. They prefer not to be bothered with the details of the project and leave it to department managers and IT to define the system requirements. Without top management support lending credibility to the project, other managers and staff often view the project as something that is nice to do but not really necessary. After all, if senior managers are not that interested why should others in the company be interested?

Problem #2: Lack of Project Manager – An external or internal project manager is often missing from these projects. It is imperative that a project manager with proven project-management skills, ERP conceptual knowledge, and ERP project experience, be given this responsibility. Many times an IT person is forced into this position, which can 'spell' disaster for the project and the IT person.

Problem #3: Lack of Project Planning – Time needs to be committed for the planning of the project. This includes all the tasks that need to be accomplished, roles and responsibilities assigned, and task assignments with completion dates. Without proper planning, the project becomes out of control and costs the company more money.

Problem #4: Lack of a Strong Executive Sponsor – At one demonstration of a chosen ERP solution, managers from different departments, such as marketing, sales, and operations, began fighting over the functionality of the system. The system had been designed without any input from these departments. It functioned well in the area of marketing but lacked functionality for sales and operations. The CEO was not happy because what he had envisioned was not what he was viewing. The project was lacking a strong executive project sponsor. The sponsor must be someone who not only performs the role of sponsor, but also understands his role *and* has time to dedicate to the project.

Problem #5: Lack of Well-defined Project Scope – A well-defined project scope is imperative to succeeding with an ERP project and keeping a 'rein' on the budget. Without this, the scope of the project will grow, increasing the amount of monies, time, and people required to complete the project. Don't leave the Project Scope definition to the IT department! Recognize that this ERP project is a business project that requires the participation of department managers and users.

Problem #6: Lack of Infrastructure Study – Many times, these projects are begun without first doing an infrastructure study to see if the current network and databases will support current and future demand and usage patterns for the system. It is surprising how many companies do not consider the hardware equipment needs until after the ERP project has been started. This can be a very costly error that can delay or stop the project.

Problem #7: Use Consultants Where They are Needed – There are 3 types of consultants that may be needed during an ERP project: application, technical, and management. Consultants are there to give you advice and direction. Do not turn the project over to them and expect them to do all the work. This will cost you in terms of money, time, and ownership of the system! Consultants have their place on the project team and can be a source of information to help the team implement the system.

Implementations of ERP systems are complex projects that usually involve major changes to the internal business processes. Don't underestimate the money, time, people, and effort required to successfully complete an ERP system. Avoid 'project scope creep' by following the project plan. Address problems, as they occur – not later.

Ronnie: Ellen, you explained that answer so well that I can only add this. Poor project planning is one of the leading causes for implementation cost over-runs. 3 critical elements of the project plan area:

(1) Well defined project identifying the scope,

(2) Cost/benefit analysis, and
(3) Timeline.

Too often the scope of the project is not well defined. "Implement the software and train the users!" is the battle cry the project team hears and that is their focal point. The scope to the project increases as the project progresses. Many times the project expands with little or no thought being given to the additional cost or resources required. Each increase may only be minor, but as they begin to accumulate, the time required for implementation and the cost of the project increases. Expanding the scope of the project is not necessarily a bad thing, but expanding the scope without recognizing the additional costs can and will result in cost overruns. Before expanding the scope, the additional costs versus the additional benefits should be examined.

Many implementation projects begin without a cost/benefit analysis. This can result in some very unpleasant surprises for the company. The expectations of the end results may be higher than the actual benefit that will be derived and the cost may greatly exceed the anticipated cost. The cost of training and the cost of using consultants are 2 costs that are often overlooked completely or are underestimated in the initial planning stages. This results in adding to the cost overrun of the project.

Another major cause of cost overruns is the lack of check points for progress. A timeline is an ideal tool for keeping the project on schedule. The timeline should consist of dates for specific tasks to be started and completed. The timeline should include all the tasks required for implementation, including but not limited to, software selection, prototyping and testing, user training, data conversion, and cut over dates.

Question: What are some of the direct benefits of ERP?

Ronnie: The ability to share information is one of the major benefits of an ERP system. Information can be viewed and used by numerous users without duplication of data input. Automation of many of the business processes assists in providing more timely information for users.

Data accuracy improves as a result of less errors when duplication of data input is eliminated. Uniform methods of identifying items and inputting data are developed. This improves data accuracy.

Another benefit is the availability of information on a more timely basis. The ability to retrieve information online in a real time manner allows management to react to situations in a more timely manner with more up to the minute information. Information can be accumulated rapidly, allowing more time for data analysis before making a decision.

Normally, either before or during a new implementation, a review of the current business practices and work flows is performed. The review normally results in improved business practices or work flows.

Ellen: Yes, Ronnie, and let me elaborate a little further. I can see 5 direct benefits of ERP.

Benefit #1: Integration of Data – Data can be entered once and shared by departments within an organization. Duplication of data is eliminated. This cuts down on the number of data errors that can occur when data is maintained on paper forms.

Benefit #2: Real time information throughout all functional areas of a company – Everyone within the company can gain access to critical up-to-date information that applies to their job responsibilities. For example, a customer sales representative can check on the status of a customer order by accessing that information online. The purchasing manager can check on what purchases have been received and which purchase orders are still open and pending. Senior management can get up-to-date information, as to the financial 'health' of the company, so they can make better management decisions.

Benefit #3: Improves data accuracy and standardization across the organization – When functional areas are responsible for their 'own' data, they usually maintain it their 'way'. No rules or procedures for entering the data are applied. For example, the organization might not have established an inventory numbering scheme. This leads to confusion because the purchasing department may order part #123 but the receiving clerk may call it part #XYZ and the inventory department may identify it as another number. For any ERP solution to provide accurate data, they must standardize rules for identifying, entering, and maintaining that data within the system.

Benefit #4: Forces 'best practice' standards to be applied throughout the organization – An ERP solution forces 'best practice' standardization to be established by the fact that each of the functional modules has it built within the applications itself. The manner in which data flows and transactions are processed within the applications dictates that an organization establishes 'best practice' standardized procedures.

Benefit #5: Analysis and reporting can be used for planning – As data is entered into the system and maintained within databases, management can access the data for analysis quickly and efficiently. Management can use historical data to look at trends, compare sales activities, pinpoint problem areas, and exam the financial 'health' of the company.

An example of how management can use data to help them make decisions can be illustrated by 'looking' at what happened in one company. A well-established mold machine company was experiencing a slow-down in orders. The manager had taken measures within the company to avoid having to lay off his people. He recognized that experienced, skilled tool-die people are not replaced easily. A customer approached him to quote a job for them. He based his quote on the work the company had previously done for the customer. The customer accepted the quote and issued a purchase order for the work to be done. A job order was issued to the shop floor; the order was produced and shipped to the customer. When time came to invoice the job to the customer, the manager noted that he had lost a substantial amount of monies on the job. He could not understand how that happened, as there were no variations in material, labor, or overhead. Upon examination of the labor reports generated from data entered into the system for this job, the manager noted that it had taken the shop 3 times as long to complete the job. Armed with the reports, he assembled his people and asked why this had occurred. It seemed that the workers were shifting the job from one process to another, taking much longer to complete the job in an effort to keep busy and avoid being laid off. The employees did not realize that they had actually 'hurt' themselves and the company, causing the manager to lose money.

The ability to analyze the data and get to the root cause of the problems is one of the major benefits to an ERP solution. It prevents management and others from chasing numbers by allowing more time to analyze those numbers, resulting in the ability to make better management decisions.

Question: How can ERP help our company make more money?

Ronnie: Using ERP as a tool to better manage your business will result in improving profits. Management can make improved financial decisions because they have better and more readily available data. Proper use of an ERP system can assist an enterprise to become more productive and efficient, thus more profitable.

Ellen: Exactly, Ronnie, in the past when senior managers needed to make a financial decision, they often had to wait several days to receive a report containing the necessary information. By then the report was already outdated and often erroneous. The ability to gain access to information online and in realtime allows management to keep a finger on the pulse of the company. Inefficiencies, production bottlenecks, inventory levels, escalation in costs, and reduction of revenues can be analyzed quickly.

One company I worked with had enormous inventory problems. No one knew what items were in stock; the numbers gathered, during physical inventory counts, were always inaccurate. After implementing ERP, they were forced to establish inventory controls and procedures for the system to give them accurate data. By accumulating the data, they were able to analyze inventory purchases, usage, sales, and turnover ratios. By establishing inventory procedures and controls, the company was able to reduce their inventory by 25%, which in turn lowered inventory costs, optimized inventory stock levels, and improved customer service.

Another area where an ERP solution can help a company make more money is in the area of sales. When a sales quote is generated, managers can base their quote on the most up-to-date information regarding material costs, labor, and overhead. Prior to submitting the quote to a customer, managers can look at data pertaining to similar jobs that the company performed in the past. They can look at the current material costs based on the last purchased price of the items. They can look at work center rates to determine how long it will take to produce an item, and the labor/overhead costs associated with these work centers. By having access to this data, managers can submit a quotation where the company will make a profit instead of a loss.

These are a couple of areas in which an ERP solution can help a company be more efficient, productive, and profitable.

Question: How can ERP help our company cut costs?

Ellen: There are many areas where ERP can help a company cut costs. ERP can provide senior management with the financial, analytical reports that they need on which to base executive decisions. In the past, it could take several days for executives to receive the information they needed to make a decision; but with the ERP system they have ready access to this data.

The ability to set up budgets within the ERP system and compare each month if the company is staying within the planned budget can help the CEO and CFO make financial decisions that are based on actual numbers, not estimates.

Tracking product cost – estimated against actual – can help to assess whether a company needs to increase the selling price of an item, improve the production of the item, or discontinue an item.

Having access to product information, up-to-date purchase information, and costing data, gives the company the ability to submit a quote at a profit, yet remain competitive.

Accurate inventory numbers can be analyzed and stock levels set thus reducing the amount of inventory that is held in-house. In some cases, companies experienced a 25% reduction in their inventory thus freeing up that money to be used elsewhere in the organization.

There are other areas where ERP can help to cut costs. I have only mentioned a few of the more notable ones for the purpose of discussion.

Ronnie: Yes, Ellen, as you stated, using ERP as a management tool to make better decisions will help eliminate or reduce cost. If ERP is properly implemented, elimination of duplication of work will result. Operational performance efficiencies will improve. Improved and more timely information is provided for decision making.

At one company I worked with, we implemented a cycle count program to identify and eliminate inventory accuracy problems. The resulting benefits included allowing inventory to be reduced by more than 20%, improving customer order fill rates by 35%, reducing size of stock room by 20%, and eliminating quarterly inventories. Quarterly inventories had been required just to correct the records in the database and to give the finance department a secure feeling that the quarter numbers reported were accurate. With the improvements to inventory accuracy, our outside auditing firm removed the requirement that we conduct a full inventory at fiscal year-end for reporting purposes. They accepted the inventory records and performed periodic spot checks to verify our cycle count results. The cost associated with conducting a full inventory plus the loss incurred by the forced stoppage of production to perform the inventory, was substantial, but all were eliminated.

Question: Does ERP give better numbers to run the business?

Ronnie: ERP itself does not give better numbers. If implemented properly, using ERP as a management tool will result in better numbers to manage the business. However, this is dependant on several factors. Remember, ERP is just a tool; data input into the system must be accurate. The numbers from ERP are only as good as the information put into the system, thus the old cliché, "garbage in, garbage out".

ERP will provide the numbers in a more timely manner. If properly used, ERP will also result in one set of numbers to run the business. In many companies there are several different sets of numbers being used to run the business. I have worked with several companies where the answer to questions such as, "what are the inventory levels?", "what is the shipping plan?", or "how did the company perform?" would depend on who you were talking with or what department you are asking. On one of my first visits to one company, I asked the materials manager and the plant accounting manager these questions in separate conversations. I received considerably different answers. Even more confusing was that neither had given the same number that I had derived from the financials reported for the month. Yet, each had data to support their numbers. This is not uncommon, and it makes managing a business and making good decisions very difficult.

Using ERP systems effectively should result in more accurate information on a more timely basis. The information can be shared more easily with others within the organization. This should allow for improved decisions, which in turn should result in better numbers.

Ellen:	Yes, Ronnie, you mentioned the old saying "garbage in, garbage out" and it certainly applies to ERP. If the data is not maintained accurately and data collection procedures are not established, reports will not give 'good' numbers. The accuracy of the numbers is dependent upon the human who types the data into the system.
Question:	Does ERP reduce the head count needed for an organization?
Ellen:	ERP usually does not reduce an organization's head count. When an organization embarks on an ERP implementation, employees often react negatively. They view the ERP solution as a threat to their jobs and the manner in which they 'work'. There is no doubt that an ERP solution will replace 'old' processes with 'new' processes. In some cases, job positions are eliminated due to the implementation of ERP; however, new job

positions are also created. Individuals are usually shifted to fill these new positions.

It is extremely important that senior management keep the lines of communication open in order to calm this 'fear'. Everyone within the enterprise needs to know the why, what, when, and where of the ERP project. Employees need to be assured that ERP is a tool to help them fulfill their job responsibilities more efficiently. This will help to make a smooth transition when the system goes 'live'.

Ronnie: I agree with Ellen; implementation of ERP does not reduce head count. If properly implemented, a reduction of head count may occur as a result of improved operating efficiencies. However, in some cases, an increase in head count may be required as a result of the implementation. The complexity of the new system and the learning curve for becoming proficient users of the new system may require additional people. Also, many enterprises undergo business "re-engineering" prior to and during implementation. Additional head count may be required due to this "re-engineering".

Question: What does it mean to be soft coded?

Ronnie: Soft coding is used in programming to allow a system the capability to be flexible and more functional. Soft coding usually applies to the processing of data as well as the input and output of the data. Soft coding of the output is usually seen in reports, files, and the way the video display appears. Soft coding allows the use of User

Defined Tables (UDT's) and is used in the processing of data and configuration management.

Ellen: Yes, Ronnie, and let me expound a little further. Soft coding is the opposite of hard coding. In an ERP application, hard coding can not be changed by the user; however, soft coding can be changed. Soft coding increases the functionality of the ERP solution by adding flexibility to the system. Soft coding applies to output, input and data processing.

Every company operates differently. What is important to Company A may not apply to Company B. One of these areas is the method in which Company A wants to track sales revenue. Company A wants to know how much sales revenue is generated by product line. Company B may want to track sales revenue by customer class. Configuration settings of an ERP system can be saved to memory and allow each company to operate the same program tailored to their needs. The ability to change configuration settings and other variables within the ERP solution increases the user friendliness of the system.

Soft coding can also be used to develop individual menus for each user, design screen displays, and online reports. This adds functionality to the ERP solution, limits the need to customize the application, adds variety to the solution, and keeps check on the integrity of the data flowing into the system databases.

Question: What is the ROI of an ERP system? How does one go about calculating it?

Ellen: There is no doubt that an ERP system requires a huge investment. Senior management often requires the IT manager to justify expenditures by showing them an ROI (return on investment) prior to authorizing projects. ROI for an ERP system is usually calculated during the system selection process as a means to justify the purchase, implementation, training, and maintenance investment.

ROI for an ERP system is best described as a mathematical technique to determine the benefits an organization will receive from the purchase and implementation of an ERP system. One of the methods used to calculate ROI is cost/benefit analysis. All of the costs associated with the ERP system need to be identified. These would include the purchase price, the costs of implementation, training, maintenance, equipment, and any miscellaneous costs associated with the project. These costs are then compared against the estimated savings the organization perceives as receiving from the system, such as increased customer service, operational efficiency, and inventory reduction.

Another technique for calculating ROI is the payback method. The payback method focuses on the amount of time it will take for the system to pay for itself. The formula for doing this calculation is simple and straightforward ((payback period = original net investment / (annual net revenue + depreciation)).

Regardless of the technique used to calculate ROI, organizations need to realize that they will not see a return on the investment immediately. The ROI will be realized after the system has been in place for a number of months; however, the organization can experience benefits from the system in terms of better integration and enhanced technology.

It is important to keep in mind that ROI calculations are based on assumptions and anticipated reduction in expenses plus increased revenue.

Ronnie: The ROI is often used to justify an expenditure. With ERP systems, the ROI is also used to measure how well an ERP system is performing or has been implemented. The cost/benefit analysis is generally the basis used for calculating the ROI.

The "real" ROI calculation for ERP systems is very difficult because so many of the benefits for the system are qualitative rather than quantitative. ROIs are based on assumptions, not facts. It is easy to identify cost associated with the project such as the cost of the software, the expense for training, and the cost of consultants. But it is not easy to put dollar figures to the benefits derived from the system. How much gain to operating efficiency will there be? This is very dependent on the human systems that feed and support the ERP system. How much is improved customer service levels worth? Will there be additional sales volume as a result of improved service? This can only be estimated, so a real figure for an exact calculation is impossible.

Ellen, let's revisit the payback method for calculating ROI and maybe I can clarify one point. The payback period method calculates the time it will take for a new investment to pay for itself. To calculate the payback period, 3 items are required: (1) the original investment, (2) the annual after-tax earnings, and (3) the depreciation. The original investment is divided by the sum of the annual after-tax earnings plus depreciation.

Question: For what types of situations or environments would ERP be a poor choice?

Ronnie: Remembering that ERP is more than software, ERP is a good choice for almost any situation or environment. Not all situations or environments would require the use of software or computerization. Enterprises with highly repetitive stable process flows may not require use of computers. There are some opinions that ERP is not suited for environments that are characterized by undisciplined or highly unorganized work flows and processes. For an ERP system to function in this type of environment would be difficult. The choice of utilizing ERP in these situations would be a good choice because increased discipline and organization would normally result. However, if discipline and organization do not result, then ERP would not work in this environment. Data integrity would be lacking. There would be no confidence in the information or system. This type of environment would be a bad fit for ERP.

Ellen:

Yes, Ronnie, every organization has its own 'personality'. This 'personality' flows from senior management to the guy who sweeps the shop floor. In some cases, the 'personality' of the organization does not lend itself to ERP. It is important that organizations examine and determine what type of 'personality' they have.

An ERP system is a people system. Its success or failure lies with the people within an organization. What is the general attitude displayed by the company toward ERP? Is it viewed as simply a data collection and storage tool? Is it considered to be an IT project? Do users blame IT when problems occur? How does senior management view ERP? Does senior management know and understand the true meaning of ERP?

If an organization's 'personality' is reflected negatively in these questions, then ERP would be a poor choice. Rather than being an asset to the company, the ERP system would be considered a huge liability. The quality of the data and maintenance of the data would be non-existent, thereby, making the simplest of reports useless.

Question:

How does e-business fit in with ERP? How does it affect my business?

Ronnie:

ERP and e-business can go hand in hand if that is the desire of the company. The number of businesses combining ERP and e-business increases everyday. When discussing ERP and e-business compatibility, it is important not to confuse e-business and e-commerce. Think of e-business as being the total process of conducting business electronically; the promoting, marketing, and selling of the products or services of the enterprise. e-commerce can be thought of as a subset of e-business, the electronic transactions portion of e-business. ERP vendors continue to increase their Internet strategies. Because most companies do not want to expose their entire ERP systems on the Internet, ERP systems must provide Internet functionality as well as traditional functionality and operate on different operating platforms. To satisfy this need for interaction with the Internet, ERP developers are using a modular approach or an enterprise approach. The modular approach offers Internet solutions for specific functional modules. The enterprise approach seeks to make the enterprise 100% Internet enabled, providing Internet capability for all functional modules.

E-business will have a dramatic influence on ERP in the future. How e-business affects your business depends on how much effect you are willing to allow it to have. Some businesses have not seen a need for e-business. Other companies are not comfortable with utilizing the Internet to a great extent due to security issues and other related problems. Depending upon the nature of your business, use of the Internet could range from no effect at all to having your total ERP system operating on the Internet. E-business can be utilized for presenting catalogs, product information, and other useful ways to promote products or services across the Internet even if conducting buying or selling transactions is not desirable for any reason. Rule of thumb would be to use the Internet capabilities to the fullest extent of the comfort level of the company.

Cibres

CIEB

For more information on the CIBRES e-business certification program (CIEB) check out the cibres website. (www.cibres.com)

The National Commission on Excellence in education released the following statement, "Learning is the indispensable investment required for success in the 'information age' we are entering". The need for e-business education for your business enterprise will continue to increase. Educational organizations will need to expand their educational offerings. The CIBRES organization is developing a certification program for e-business professionals, CIEB standing for Certified Implementer of E-business, which will be available in early 2002.

Ellen: That's right Ronnie; ERP systems were designed to integrate various departments within an organization. These functional modules such as accounting, distribution, manufacturing, human resources, and payroll were integrated with each other, but remained within the confines of the organization itself. Neither customers nor vendors could access the data.

With the advent of the Internet, ERP vendors have seen the need to extend their ERP software beyond the traditional four walls of an organization. The Internet has changed the fundamental way companies do business. Customers are demanding the ability to access their suppliers' management software to track orders and information. An end user wants to go straight into a distributor's system over the Internet and see whether a product is in stock before he orders it. Customers want to see the status of their orders. Distributors want to check on the production status of items. The Internet has made all of this possible. The connectivity between ERP, SCM (Supply Chain Management) and CRM must be integrated within the software solution.

With e-business, a customer can log onto your CRM system to place an order. The order is then processed by the CRM system. The system checks and validates the customer. If all is well, the order can be fulfilled. The order automatically goes to the SCM system which checks inventory required to fill the order. If there isn't enough material to fill the order, the ERP system is notified that material needs to be ordered or produced. The ERP system processes the order and prepares the shipping papers. The ERP system alerts the SCM system that the order is ready to ship. The SCM system alerts the freight carriers that the shipment is ready to be picked up for delivery. The information is then relayed back to the financial part of the ERP to send out confirmation of the shipment and process the invoice.

For this to work over the Internet, each of these systems needs to integrate with the other. Many ERP vendors are including integration tools with their ERP solution to make this possible. SAP, for example, has its own business application interfaces.

E-business has opened a whole new avenue for doing business over the Internet. When implemented correctly, e-business can expand an organization's business beyond the boundaries of its four walls.

Question: Okay, I am convinced, ERP could do great things for our company. What is the best way to get started?

Ellen:

Cibres

The *'ERP: A-Z Implementer's Guide for Success'* contains a detailed chapter on how to conduct an ERP planning session for your organization. CIBRES item number 4516.

The first step is planning. No project should begin without proper planning. Planning is the key to any successful ERP project. A well-defined project plan should be developed. The plan should list all the tasks needed to complete the project. Based on the project plan, form a project team. The team should include individuals from all the functional areas within the organization. Make sure everyone understands his or her role and responsibilities in connection with the project.

Presenting the project plan to senior management and getting their support is critical. Without this support, the project is doomed for failure before it even begins.

Ronnie: Ellen, this reminds me of a quote from Mae West, "Knowing what you want is the first step toward getting it" —and that's correct in this situation also. The first step in the process is to decide if ERP is right for your company. Decide why you want to implement a new ERP system. Just because all your competitors are doing it or just because it seems to be the right thing to do is not reason enough. Remember, this will be an expensive adventure and will require changes to your current way of doing business. People are reluctant to change unless they have a reason to change. The decision to implement an ERP system must be based on compelling reasons. During this period, you may decide to use an outside source to assist with evaluating your enterprise's current situation to determine if there is reason enough to move forward with an implementation.

After the compelling reason has been identified, top management support, approval, and commitment must be obtained. It is useless to start the project if there is not a total commitment from top management. Some ERP education may be required prior to obtaining the needed commitment. Next a project team should be established. This project team will expand as the project grows, but this core group will set the tone for the entire implementation process. A project planning session should be held to map out the project. Expect the project planning session to last as long as several days. As you stressed, Ellen, properly planning the project is a key to successful implementation. The project team should develop a Vision and a Mission statement for the project.

A cost/benefit analysis should be performed as part of the project plan. A timeline for starting and completing the project should be established. ERP education for the project team members should be provided in the early stages of the project.

Question: What is the best ERP system on the market?

Ellen: There is no 'one size fits all' when it comes to ERP systems. The best ERP system on the market is the ERP system that meets at least 95% of a company's critical business functions. It should fit in well with the company's strategic business plan and allow for future technological growth.

Ronnie:

Sly
Many unethical practices exist within the ERP industry. These poor practices have been documented on the CIBRES website.

Good question; but, as Ellen stated, there is no definitive answer here. It is important to understand that the best software on the market may not be the best software for your company. There are over 1000 ERP software packages on the market at any given time. Currently, SAP has the largest market share for ERP software, followed by Oracle, JD Edwards, PeopleSoft, and QAD, just to name a few. This is not meant to endorse or detract from any one of the software vendors. Each software package has its own advantages and disadvantages.

Many enterprises think the bigger the software package the better. Others feel that if it is more expensive, it must be better. The key question about the software should be, "Will it fulfill my business' needs?" A good examination of the needs of your business is necessary prior to deciding upon a software package. You may want an outside party to assist with the evaluation of your needs and the software to be considered. Be cautious! Any outside source you may choose to use must be impartial in regards tosoftware vendors.

3

What's it going to take?

Successful ERP does not happen by chance. Education and good planning is essential for its implementation and use. Most companies spend a lot of money trying to implement ERP. Spending millions of dollars is not uncommon. Often in the early stages companies will underestimate the costs for hardware, software, consultation, or maintenance. When companies sense that they are falling behind schedule and budget they often times bypass important implementation steps, consequently leading to circumstances that will later plague the company with problems. An ERP system must display the right information to be effective. That means that people must input the correct information. That can only happen with the right education and training.

In this chapter the reader will learn ...

1. How do ERP vendors price software?
2. What is a modification?
3. What are the hardware needs?
4. How much money will it cost?
5. What are the components of an ERP implementation?

Question: It sounds like the bigger companies all use ERP software. Can a smaller company like mine be successful with it?

Ellen: All companies, whether large or small, have the same basic business functions and needs. A small company provides customers with a product or service, produces or purchases that product, fills the order, invoices the customer, collects payments for goods sold, etc.

ERP is applicable to all companies regardless of size. ERP systems are designed to adapt to small, mid-market and large companies. Made2Manage and Visual Manufacturing are 2 systems that fit the small to medium (SME) companies. SAP, Oracle, and Peoplesoft are designed to meet the needs of larger companies who may require multi-lingual, multi-location capabilities.

It is important to every company, who is choosing an ERP system, to follow a proven system selection process. This will help to ensure that the final choice is the best one that can be made because it is based on whether the ERP solution can provide for the company's critical business criteria.

Ronnie: Yes, Ellen, and most large companies either have implemented ERP systems or are planning an ERP implementation. But ERP can be utilized by any size and type of company. Small companies may not require all the "bells and whistles" that larger companies require. It is important for any size company to chose the correct software for their business, and to determine what functional modules are needed to properly run the business. Fewer modules may be required for a small company.

Implementation time and costs are normally reduced proportionately depending on size of the company. However, depending on the requirements the small company may have, the costs and time may rival those of larger companies.

Question: How much money will it cost to buy and implement an ERP system?

Ellen: The total investment needed to buy and implement an ERP system is dependent upon a number of factors. The initial software investment for purchasing the software varies from vendor to vendor. ERP vendors may base their pricing structure on which modules are to be purchased, the number of concurrent users, or the number of servers on which the solution will be installed.

Hardware equipment costs must also be considered. Most companies find that their technology infrastructure will not support the 'new' ERP system. Legacy machines need to be retired or allocated to another usage. Companies requiring 24/7 operation of the system usually experience a greater investment than companies requiring a standard 8/5 operation.

Most companies do not have people on staff with the necessary skills to implement an ERP system. They need temporary assistance from consultants.

The consultants may be provided to them by the software vendor, equipment vendor, or an outside firm. Consultant charges are usually negotiated based on the role they are to have in the project.

Training is always a necessary expenditure when implementing a 'new' ERP system. Most companies find that a 'train the trainer' approach helps to contain the costs they will incur in this area. Training costs would include the cost of the instructor as well as a fee for the class.

Ronnie: It has been my experience, Ellen, and I'm sure the same is true for you, the total cost of purchasing and implementing ERP software will vary depending on the size of the company, the complexity of the business processes, the number of functional modules installed, and the method of implementation. You can expect costs to range from $500,000 to $300 million dollars. The average cost is approximately $1 million. These costs include the cost of the software, any additional hardware that may be required, outside services, temporary employees, and the additional cost of internal employees.

You must remember that the cost of the new system does not stop with the purchase and implementation. Lease and maintenance agreements are normally spread over several years. Ongoing training and post implementation work of the project team will need to continue, thus additional cost.

Question: What are the major categories of cost for implementing an ERP system and how do we make estimates for each one?

Ellen: Category #1: Software Costs – Software costs are dependent upon the ERP vendor's pricing structure. ERP vendors have their own method for pricing the software. This is one reason why you may want to talk to the software companies and obtain information regarding their pricing of their systems. For estimating purposes, it is a good idea to make your estimated costs higher. For example, if vendors say their system costs $10,000 per module, you may want to raise the estimated figure to $15,000 per module.

Category #2: Hardware Costs – Equipment is dependent upon a number of factors. What is the current technological infrastructure of the company? What is the future technology plan for the company? Will the current machines and operating systems on those machines 'run' the new ERP system? Will the current machines give you the needed performance level required by your company? Does your company require a 24/7 operation? These are a few of the questions you need to answer when estimating the costs associated with the hardware needs of an ERP project. You can obtain hardware estimate costs after these basic questions have been examined. Talk to a reputable dealer such as IBM, Compaq, or Dell. Tell them what your anticipated equipment needs are. They will be able to provide an estimated equipment cost for your consideration.

Category #3: Data Conversion Costs – An essential key element of an ERP system is data. Your company must decide to get the data out of the 'old' system and into the 'new' system. Some companies prefer to 'key' all of the data into the 'new' system. They want to be assured that the data being entered is 'clean' and does not contain inaccuracies from the 'old' system. Of course, this requires time and people. Other companies use an interface program to download data from the 'old' system into the 'new' system. Costs associated with data conversions are dependent upon several factors. For example, how 'clean' is the data in your 'old' system? Has it been properly maintained for accuracy? Was the 'old' data entered into the system using a series of data standardization rules or was it just keyed 'in any old way'? How much data history does your company want to retain in the 'new' system? These are some of the questions that need to be answered when you're trying to estimate the costs for getting data into the 'new' system.

Category #4: Customization Costs – Normally, an ERP system will accommodate a company's needs in its 'vanilla' state; however, you may need to make some changes to the system. You should only make customizations if it is imperative to conducting business. Customizations add to the cost of the ERP system, maintenance, and upgrade costs. Programming and configuring the system could require a considerable amount of time and money.

Category #5: Maintenance and Support Fees – Most ERP vendors charge an on-going annual fee for upgrades and new releases of the system. The fee is usually calculated as a percentage of the total software purchase cost. Percentages can range from 10% - 20% per year. There will also be an ongoing maintenance cost to install the upgrades.

Category #6: Training and Education – With every new ERP system, you must include training and education. A 'train the trainer' approach has been found to be an efficient manner in which to administer initial training on the new system. Training costs will vary but it is not unusual for a company to expect to spend $1200.00 to $1500.00 per day for the trainer to come on-site to teach the class. Out-of-pocket expenses for the trainer would include travel, meals, and lodging. You may also choose to send your people to an off-site location for training. Most ERP vendors have off-site locations where they conduct training in a classroom. Costs for this type of training may be based on a class fee, per person fee, or a group fee. You will need to budget for ongoing training and education of company personnel. Allocating 25% of the initial software investment to training and education is a good starting figure.

There are other costs associated with an ERP implementation. Does your company need to hire outside consultants to help with the project? Are temporary clerical personnel needed to help with the daily activities of your business while permanent employees can help build the system? What miscellaneous software or other expenses may be incurred during the project?

Unfortunately, most companies underestimate the amount of time, people, and costs associated with an ERP system implementation. As with any project, count the cost in terms of time, people, and money before initiating the project.

Ronnie: Ellen, as you stated, software and hardware costs, education and training costs, manpower costs, and costs of consulting services are the major categories you need to consider when you estimate the costs of an ERP implementation. You should also consider post implementation costs.

You can estimate the cost of software by reviewing pricing for different software packages containing the functional modules that you anticipate needing. You can do these estimates prior to beginning any formal project, but the estimates are normally based on or revised using information obtained from the Request for Information phase of the project. Expected cost can be estimated at approximately $12,000 per module to be implemented. The cost of additional hardware is done after a review of additional hardware requirements has been performed. You should use great care not to overlook additional hardware requirements. Many projects experience cost overruns or many other problems because hardware requirements were not recognized during the investigation stages of the projects.

You can estimate the manpower costs to implement the project by breaking down the tasks to be performed into time requirements and calculating equivalent manpower hours. When you estimate manpower or resources required, do not overlook the cost of temporary resources that may be required to perform duties normally performed by project team members. Costs should also include any estimated overtime requirements.

Not all implementation projects require the use of outside consulting services. You should compare the project needs to the in-house expertise available early in the planning stages to determine if outside consulting assistance will be required and what type consulting help you need. To estimate the costs, the needs should be determined, then cost estimates can be obtained from potential consultants. Most successful projects utilize outside consulting help of one or more consultants. Generally a management consultant is utilized to assist with managing the project, identifying needs, assisting in software review and selection, and auditng the progress of the project. Some technical and application consulting may be provided by the ERP service provider as part of the software purchase agreement. Do not overlook the use of consulting services during the cost estimating process. Too often the need for outside assistance is not recognized until the project experiences some major setback. This usually results in cost overruns for the projects, due to unplanned consulting costs incurred.

One major cost that is often overlooked or hidden is the post implementation maintenance that is required. These costs may include the establishment of a help desk to assist users, on going education and training of users, upgrades to software or hardware, and additional hardware.

Question: How do ERP vendors price their software?

Ellen: ERP vendors have different methods for pricing their software. Some vendors base the pricing on a per server basis. Others base pricing on the number of concurrent users or the individual modules that may be purchased. Let's examine how one popular ERP vendor prices their system.

Due to the modular architecture of the system, a company has the benefit of licensing and implementing only the application modules that is of relevance to them. The modules for the core ERP system would include:

Suite #1: Financials – General Ledger, Accounts Payable, Accounts Receivable, Fixed Assets, and Management Accounting

Suite #2: Sales – Sales Forecasting, Sales Analysis, Sales Order Management, and Shipping

Suite #3: Logistics – Inventory Management, Purchase Management, Sub-Contracting, Physical Inventory and Cycle Control

Suite #4: Process Production – Modeling, Planning, Scheduling, and Operations

Pricing is based on the number of concurrent users. A 50 concurrent user software license would cost $300,000. This would allow access to Financials, Sales, Productions, Logistics. For each additional concurrent user $5,000 (must be purchased in blocks of 5).

Tools and Utilities – User Defined Screens, Data Drill Down, Report Writer, Workflow, Application Configurator, Notes, Common Code Help, Audit Trail, GUI Editor, Security, Formula Builder, and Default Setting Utility - $30,000 (number of licenses equal to ERP licenses)

Total cost for ERP software package: $330,000.

ERP implementation consultant costs for project manager, trainer, business consultant, and technical consultant would equal $4,200 per day. Estimated costs to provide implementation and training services would range from $125,000 to $175,000. This service estimate does not include any significant modifications or customization work. All travel and related out-of-pocket expenses will be at actual.

Maintenance and on-going support for the package is 15% of the total list price of the software ERP license. This is billed annually.

This scripted quotation is typical of what a company would receive from an ERP vendor. It varies with the pricing structure dictated by the vendor but this is a good representation of how these systems are costed. CIBRES recommends that when an ERP vendor submits a proposal for a system that the company requests that the proposal be broken into sections such as the one I just discussed. This will make it easier to analyze the costs and present it to senior management for approval.

Ronnie: Ellen, you covered that topic thoroughly. The only thing I can add is that vendor's price their software based on the complexity of the software, number of modules, technological bells and whistles offered, and service and assistance required. The number of users and the number of servers that will be used also influence the price of the software. Some rather inexpensive software may perform all the needed functions an enterprise requires. However, the more functionality required, the more costly the software and the more time consuming the implementation.

Question: What will be needed in terms of hardware? How does a company determine the size of computer that will be needed?

Ronnie: Good question to be asked up front. In many instances, software is purchased without any consideration for the hardware required. A friend of mine was involved in an implementation where she works. The project was not well planned in the beginning, and pieces were put together rather haphazardly. Software was purchased, but when it was received, it could not be loaded because the current mainframe would not support the software. Additional hardware had to be purchased, immediately causing a cost over-run. Sadly, this is not an isolated case.

Warning

Using undersized hardware to run an ERP system can lead to many frustrated users!

The determination of hardware requirements should be included in the initial planning stages and included in the cost/benefits analysis. In addition the size of computer required to operate the software, other hardware such as printers, scanners, modems, personal desktop computers, etc. may be required. Upgrades to existing equipment may be sufficient in some cases while new purchases may be required in others.

A company may use several resources to determine the hardware needs. Depending on the capabilities and expertise of the company's own IT department, these requirements may be determined by the IT staff. Software and hardware vendors and outside consultants may also be utilized to assist in determining these needs.

A needs analysis should be performed in the initial stages of the project. The needs analysis will assist in determining what users need from the system and can serve as a basis for determining the hardware needs. The size of the software, the number of transactions that will be performed, the amount of traffic or users on the system, the methods of processing data whether batch or real time, etc. all will have an impact on the size of the computer required.

Ellen: I agree, Ronnie, the technology architecture around which an ERP solution is modeled is critical. Good technology architecture can increase the scope of the solution and give it a new dimension. Over the last few years, client-server architecture has grown in its ability to support small or large ERP solutions. The architecture and alternate ways to deploy an ERP solution is detailed by the ERP vendor. The ERP vendor will furnish a company with the minimum operating requirements for their particular system. Companies should remember that these are minimum requirements. These minimum requirements usually need to be increased to achieve the level of system performance users may need.

A minimum server configuration for a typical ERP solution would consist of Pentium-II 566 MHz dual processors; 256 MB RAM; 20 GB Hard Drive; Backup etc.

Minimum client machine configuration would be Pentium 133 MHz; 32 MB RAM.

CIBRES recommends that an inventory of the current systems be performed prior to purchasing new machines. Many times, a company may have machines that could be upgraded or relocated; thereby, 'cutting' down on the investment that must go to purchase new machines.

Question: Where can I go to find out more information about all the different ERP vendors?

Ellen:

Cibres
Visit the CIBRES website for information on many different ERP vendors. Visitors will find the capability to search by name, operating systems, databases, etc...

You can find a wealth of information about ERP software vendors via the Internet. Most ERP vendors have an established website where you can find information regarding their products, services, and contacts. You may also be able to register to view a web-based demonstration of their products.

Another source of information is the CIBRES organization website www.cibres.com. The CIBRES organization maintains an ERP Vendor Chart. This chart lists the ERP vendor, annual revenue, software category (ERP, MRPII, CRM);

supported server platforms (NT, Unix, Windows, IBM); supported databases (IBM, DB2, MS SQL Server, Oracle); types of Industries (Aerospace, Chemical, Packaged goods, Foods); industrial environments (Customer Service, Discrete, Process, Make-to-stock, Make-to-order, Repetitive); and links to the vendor's website.

You may want to consult with an expert who specializes in system selections. A reputable system selection expert can save you time, money and frustration when trying to access reliable information about ERP vendors. Many times, these experts have inside knowledge about a system and can point you in the right direction very quickly.

Ronnie: Right, Ellen, there are several places to obtain information about ERP software vendors. The most comprehensive listing I am aware of is the CIBRES website. The CIBRES Comparison Chart can be viewed online. The chart compares 100 of the top software vendors. www.cio.com is another good source for information about ERP software, as well as general ERP related information. Several times, the APICS publication, "The Performance Advantage", has published a listing of ERP software vendors and included a brief description of the various products.

Question: What if the software we purchase does not match our needs? Will we need to make software modifications?

Ronnie: If the software purchased does not match your business needs, yes, modifications may be required. But a change in method of doing business may be an even better solution. The fewer modifications allowed, the better. Software modifications can be very expensive to make, depending on the programming time required. Modifications should be very well documented. The documentation should include the reasons for the modification as well as the modification itself. Every effort should be made to find a software that does match your business needs. Sometimes it may be wise to change the way you do business or some part of your business rather than performing major modifications to the software. Software modifications can become expensive to maintain and difficult to upgrade as newer versions of the software are made available.

One of the most successful implementations I have been involved with was predicated on the fact that no software modifications would be allowed. The project team was directed to review and revise the business practices for the best methods of doing business, then find a software package that would match those practices. If this could not be achieved, then the project team was to do the opposite, find a software that would perform the desired way, then change the business practices to match the software. This was based on the reasoning that if an adequate job of business methods review and software review/selection is performed, then modifications should not be required.

Any requests for modification had to be submitted to the steering committee for approval. Then the requestor had to appear before the steering committee to explain the request, explain what had been done to use the system, and why the modification was necessary. No approvals for modification were granted. Improved methods of performing business functions were developed. The software was installed and the cut-over achieved without modifications to the software. The only changes allowed were changes to the format of reports. These were not software modifications. The project was successful and the company reaped many benefits from the review of the business practices.

Ellen: Unfortunately, Ronnie, as I'm sure you have experienced, purchasing software that doesn't match their needs happens to more companies than one would think. For example, a process manufacturer purchases an ERP system that is designed for the discrete manufacturer. This can be compared to a person trying to fit a square peg into a round hole. The customizations required to adapt this software to the needs of the process manufacturer would be incredibly difficult. It would also impede the company's ability to upgrade the software in the future.

A company needs to ask themselves, "Does the software meet at least 95% of our critical needs?" As you stated, Ronnie, many times, it is not the software that needs to be modified but the business processes of the company that needs to be re-engineered. There is no doubt that any time a company talks about changing processes, people within the organization become nervous. Change management is a primary concern when implementing an ERP system.

It is wiser and more cost effective to adapt your business processes to the software than to modify the system if at all possible. Keep the modifications to a minimum.

Companies who find themselves with the wrong software solution have 3 choices:
(1) Re-engineer their business processes to match the system as much as possible;
(2) Customize the solution to match their business needs; or
(3) Throw away the solution and start over again.

Question: I have heard that having accurate data is critical for the success of an ERP system. Our data always seems inaccurate. How do we deal with that?

Ellen: Inaccurate data is problem that seems to plague many companies. It can be imported during the data conversion phase of an ERP implementation. Other causes for the existence of inaccurate data in an ERP system are:

- Human keying errors;
- Lack of data entry standards & procedures; and
- Incomplete customer, vendor, and item information.

Inaccurate data not only affects the ERP system but can also lead to disconnects within the company. For example, manufacturing can not use the bills of material from engineering because it is always wrong so manufacturing manually develops the correct bill of material consistent with how they make the product. Purchasing can not work from the MRP for ordering material because leadtimes of purchased material extend beyond the MPS from manufacturing. Senior management can not depend upon the financial reports being generated from the system because they can not rely on the 'bottom line' being calculated accurately. All of this inaccurate data causes problems throughout an organization.

Accurate data is the 'backbone' that supports the ERP system. Without accurate data, an ERP system will degrade and in time, fail. What can a company do to correct this problem?

Step #1: Set data standards and guidelines. Make sure that everyone understands them. For example, what data standards have been developed for entering items, customers, and vendors into the system?

Step #2: Develop a procedure for maintaining the BOMs and routing information. Bills of material and routing information should be maintained at a 99% accuracy. Anything less than that will create problems with planning, production, inventory and purchasing.

Step #3: Develop procedures for managing changes to the system. If everyone within an organization is allowed to make changes to the data, inaccurate data will result.

Step #4: Conduct periodic checks to make sure the data is correct. For example, take a short list of inventory items. Go out in the plant. Count the items. See if the physical count matches what the system shows. If it does, GREAT! If not, you have a problem!

These are simple preventative steps that companies should implement to help 'ward' off corrupting their ERP systems with bad data.

Ronnie: Yes, Ellen, accurate data is critical for the success of an ERP system. The old adage, "garbage in, garbage out" is true. Inaccurate data results in loss of confidence in the system by users at all level of the organization. Audits to identify inaccurate information, problem identification, and corrective actions are essential for mantaining accuracy in the system. Management needs accurate information to make informed decisions that may drastically affect the business. Customer service levels, purchasing requirements, production requirements, and staffing requirements all are adversely affected by inaccurate information. The need for accurate inventory information is critical. Inaccurate information results in inaccurate reporting of profitability.

The need for accurate information goes beyond just numbers, it also includes information regarding the addresses, phone numbers, and other contact information for employees, customers, and suppliers. Accurate bills of material and routings are not only essential for the production of the product but also for the proper costing of the product.

During implementation is a good time to "clean up" the data in the system. But once the system is implemented and cutover is complete, the accuracy of the data must be maintained. Sufficient training for the data input employees to perform their functions properly is essential. But education of these employees explaining the effects their functions have on the total system should also be provided. Period audits should be performed to check the accuracy of information in the system. Cycle counting is one method of auditing inventory records and includes correct storage location, part number, part description, as well as accurate count information. Similiar methods should be utilized to perform audits of vendor, customer, and employee information. Audits of bills of materials and routings should also be performed.

Question: Will our company need to hire additional people?

Ellen: Whether a company needs to hire additional people depends upon their internal resources. A few companies have found that they were able to successfully implement their ERP system without hiring additional people.

A company may recognize that they do not have people with the technology or project skills necessary to implement the system. Consultants, technical or temporary clerical help are examples of the types of people that a company may need to hire during the implementation phase of the project. These individuals can help permanent employees during the implementation in a number of ways. They can fill the working gaps and 'free' up a company's best people to concentrate on the ERP implementation project.

Once a system goes 'live' a company may require additional IT people for programming, report writing, network or system support, and maintenance.

The need to hire additional people is a need that every company must address. This should be part of the planning phase of the project. Without skilled people being dedicated to the project, companies soon find their ERP implementation project missing deadlines, experiencing "project scope creep" and the bottom dollar line growing.

Ronnie: Yes Ellen, after implementation, there may be a need to hire additional people to obtain the skills and expertise required to operate or to support the new system. Many companies do not have people with the required skills or knowledge, so additional people must be hired.

Question: How many consultants will it take?

Ronnie: The need for assistance from a consultant and the number of consultants required will vary from company to company, depending upon the expertise of the company employees. Also, the type of consultant to be used will vary. Consultants can be classified as management, application, and technical consultants. Most consultants can provide one of these services but not all 3. Many consultants may be able to provide 2 of the services, but it is rare that one consultant can effectively provide management, application, and technical services.

Most software vendors provide or offer technical support as well as assistance with applications. When selecting and purchasing the software, it is wise to get a clarification on these services. How many hours are included in the purchase price and what is really included. Some software vendors also will recommend other consultants to assist with the implementation. They are familiar with these consultants and the consultants are familiar with their products. However, it is wise to be cautious when selecting a consultant, even ones that are recommended by your software vendor. Be sure you understand the relationship between the software vendor or service provider and the consultant.

Companies that have complex business process flows or large complex installations may require substantial consulting assistance. Also, a project that has a weak project team or project team leader usually requires the help of a consultant. How many and what kind of consultants will be required will differ from company to company, implementation to implementation, based on the in house skills, type of implementation strategy being used, and other factors relevant to individual companies.

Ellen: Let me add, Ronnie, during the early implementation-planning phase of the ERP project, is when a company should consider whether they need to hire a consultant. Companies should have a clear definition of the role that the consultant needs to fill during the ERP project. It is important that the consultant(s) assist them with the ERP project and not do it for them. Consultants can provide companies with a wide variety of services, including project management. As Ronnie stated, there are 3 basic types of consultants: Management, Application and Technical. Let me explain the duties of each type of consultant.

Application consultants focus on the functionality of the software application. They educate, demonstrate, and configure the software based on the business process flow of the software.

Management consultants may fill the role of project manager, help with business process re-engineering and examine the company's internal controls or procedures. Management consultants focus on the management issues of the company. They provide direction to the core team in managing the project by pointing out possibly 'pitfalls' to the project.

Technical consultants focus on technical issues of the ERP project. These technical issues may concern the software application, database conversion, customizations, interfaces, operating systems, hardware systems, software installations or communication protocols. The technical consultants work closely with the application and management consultants.

The number of consultants a company may require and what role the consultant fulfills are decisions each company must decide. The benefit a company derives from a consultant depends upon the consultant and a company's ability to utilize the consultant's advice.

Question: How does one begin the process of education for ERP? Who should be involved? What types of classes?

Ronnie: It has been stated that for every $1 spent on education, a savings of $1000 may be realized during the implementation and use of an ERP system. The first step in the education process is to determine who needs the education, how much education is needed, and what kind of education is needed. To make these determinations, the organizational structure and the expertise that currently exists in the organization should be examined. Everyone from top management to end users should be involved.

Classes should be provided for basic ERP education and also for training of how to use the software that has been selected. Most everyone in the organization should receive education on the basic ERP concepts. After the basic concepts are understood, education of each of the ERP functional modules should be provided for anyone involved with the use of any particular functional module. Classes in business management techniques may also be included.

Top management should receive basic ERP education prior to the determination that an implementation project is required. This allows top management to understand what ERP is, what to benefits to expect from an ERP implementation, the costs and pitfalls of an ERP implementation, and to understand what will be required from them for the implementation to be successful.

After the decision to proceed with the ERP implementation, the core project team members and the critical stakeholders should receive basic ERP education as well as training to use the functional modules. One of the most commonly made and most costly mistakes made during an implementation is the lack of training of the end users to properly use the software. How much training is too much? Users should be trained until they are comfortable that they can perform their functions properly with the new software. I commonly use the phrase, "Train the user until they beg you to go live" so they can use the system.

Ellen: I agree, Ronnie. Just as an engineer needs education and training to build a bridge or design a skyscraper, anyone involved with an ERP project needs education and training. The level of the education/training would depend upon a person's involvement with the project. It is not unusual for companies to embark on an ERP implementation project with little or no knowledge of what ERP is, how to manage an ERP project or what it takes to complete the project successfully.

An excellent starting point for ERP education and training is the CIBRES organization. CIBRES offers education and training for ERP professionals, individuals and companies. The

CIBRES publication, *ERP: A-Z Implementer's Guide for Success* is a 750-page hardback book. It contains all the information to help a company successfully implement ERP. It provides basic ERP concepts that can be applied to ERP projects. It can be ordered directly online from the CIBRES organization on their website.

Besides offering ERP education and training, the CIBRES organization offers ERP certification seminars and exams. Individuals, who have earned the CIERP (Certified Implementer of Enterprise Resource Planning) certification, have demonstrated their knowledge and understanding by passing a 240-question certification examination. This type of training can an invaluable asset to a company both before, during and after the ERP project has been completed.

A company must decide what, who, how, and where in regard to the educational needs of its organization. Every company is different because of the skill levels of their people, the type of software solution chosen, and the project scope. It is recommended that a company develop an on-going continuous education and training program for updating technical skills, IT, or providing training for new users on the system.

Question: What are the key procedures that people and top management should follow to ensure a successful ERP system?

Ellen: In a manufacturing facility, quality control is vital. A company can not afford to produce and ship substandard material to customers. Quality control programs help to ensure that no substandard material goes out of the facility to a customer. It takes effort on the part of the company to make sure that processes, procedures, and controls are established to monitor the overall quality of a product.

The same principal applies to an ERP system. A company needs to implement a total quality management plan for their ERP system. A TQM plan helps to maintain the 'health' of an ERP system. The following is a list of the key points of a TQM plan:

Leadership – For an ERP system to be successful, management needs to be involved before, during, and after an implementation. One or two senior managers need to stay involved with the system; resolving problems, allocating resources, and providing the figure of authority to others within the organization.

Commitment – Senior management must first and foremost be committed to making the ERP system successful.

Continuous Improvement – Establish a continuous improvement plan for the ERP system. Continuous improvement is often not applied to an ERP system. It is generally assumed that once the system goes 'live' nothing else needs to be done. Continuous improvement is a method for learning how to use the system and adjust business processes to match the software's capabilities. This will help to eliminate unnecessary modifications to the software.

Total Involvement – It is important that management, department heads, and end users are involved with the system. This involvement helps smooth the organization's transition from the legacy system to the 'new' ERP system.

Training and education – Companies need to establish an ERP training program. An ERP training program is company specific. It shows how to use the software for specific business processes.

Ownership – The ERP system is a people system. End users need to realize that this is their system. Strong end user ownership helps to make an ERP system successful. Too many times the IS department is thought to 'own' the system. This causes endless problems and in some cases, results in the 'death' of the system.

Performance Measures – It is important that a series of performance measures be used to make sure that the people, processes, and technology are aligned with each other. If one of these support structures fail, the ERP system will collapse if the problem is not addressed.

Data Integrity and Accuracy – Periodic random checks of the data should be done. If the end users and management can not trust the data, the ERP system will cease to be used.

These are a few of the key things that should be done to help ensure a successful ERP system. Many companies use visual quality tools or electronic monitoring tools to assess the system. Regardless of the method used, a company should keep a 'close eye' on their ERP system. TQM can help a company do this.

Ronnie: Well, Ellen, you answered that question so thoroughly that the only thing I can possibly add is what a former Texas football coach Darrel Royal said, "Luck is what happens when preparation meets opportunity". Preparation is key to successful ERP systems. One key element of the preparation is education and training. Basic ERP education for everyone involved, including top management, to project team members, end users, etc. Top management must understand how the business is really run and must understand how to use the information from the ERP system.

In addition to education, another essential element of preparation is project planning. One quote credited to Yogi Berra is, "You got to be careful if you don't know where you are going you may not get there". The project plan provides direction to where the company wants to go and includes some instruction as to how to get there.

Question: What are some things a company should do after the ERP system is fully installed?

Ronnie: Once the systems are converted and the "go live" has taken place, an audit and comparison of the data should be performed to ensure that accurate information is being received from the new system. If, prior to cut-over, the testing of the software and data integrity was performed sufficiently, the results of the audits should reveal no surprises. But, surprises do happen, and companies must be prepared to react to take corrective actions to these situations. Until this step is complete and the results are acceptable, I do not consider the system as being fully installed.

ERP should be thought of as a journey, not a destination. Normally once the "go live" transition is complete, most companies consider the implementation complete. That is one of the reasons so many companies fail to reap the desired benefits of their ERP implementations. The "go live" is really only the beginning. Documenting the system is very crucial, but is so often overlooked. Documentation is more than just the user manuals provided by the software vendor. Documentation also includes how the company does business and how the software and the company business practices function together.

Continued maintenance of the system is required. Continuation of training and retraining of users is essential. Some users will leave the company, others will change jobs within the company. For various reasons, there will be a need for continued training.

Continuous Improvement and Total Quality Management programs should become a part of the ERP process. These concepts are generally accepted for manufacturing processes in industry today, but companies should seek ways to make them a part of the ERP system. Ways to improve the system's performance and data integrity are keys to ERP survival. Management must continue to support the ERP system, not to view it as just another software that has been installed or as a completed project that can be taken off the board. As Albert Einstein said, "The important thing is not to stop questioning."

Ellen: Right, Ronnie, a misconception that many organizations have is that once the ERP is fully implemented, the system should operate as any other piece of software. They fail to realize that the ERP system is not like other software. Other software, such as Auto Cad or Microsoft Office, aids employees to be more efficient and productive; however, these software packages are not used to 'run' the business. The ERP system contains all the company's business transactions and financial data needed to operate their company.

CIBRES also recommends that an organization develop a TQM program for the ERP system. TQM involves everyone within the organization and 'forces' shared ownership of the system. This increases the overall value of the ERP system. Let's examine some of the areas where TQM will help a company maintain their ERP system and ensure data integrity.

Management Involvement – It is a recommended best practice standard that at least one or two senior managers stay closely involved with the implementation and maintenance of the ERP system. Senior managers have the authority and power to resolve conflicts that may arise either with the system or with the end users. They can allocate resources needed to correct problems as they occur.

Continuous Improvement – Continuous improvement is a concept rarely applied to ERP systems. Most companies do not see the 'need' for continuous improvement when it comes to the ERP system. The company tries to 'fix' the system through modifications to the system. It is much more advantageous for a company to learn how to use the ERP system and adjust their processes to the system instead of making unnecessary software modifications.

For example, one company took 3 months to implement their ERP system. Over the course of the next 12 to 18 months, the staff 'dug' into the system. They learned everything they needed to know to do their jobs within the confines of the system. They applied continuous improvement methodology to the system and learned to work with the system instead of making unnecessary modifications. The staff learned that they could use the system as it was configured except for some reports that needed to be created. This company utilizes 100% of the ERP system. They used financial and costing information that was produced from the system's database to make management decisions. They knew that they could depend upon the data for accuracy.

Another company spent 2 years implementing and modifying their ERP system. Their philosophy was one of "the system is not going to dictate how to run our business". The result was that although the system was somewhat functional, the company only utilized maybe 25% of the system. Many of the documents were still manually produced outside of the ERP system. Senior management did not use the financial reports because they could not depend upon the figures being accurate.

Ownership – It is absolutely vital that the end users realize that this is their 'system'. They must take ownership of the ERP system. The ownership of the system should not be delegated to the IS department. This can result in a barrage of problems with everyone blaming IT for system problems or inadequacies. Without the support of management, end users and the ERP vendor, the ERP system will suffer a slow death. No system can survive without this type of support.

Performance Measures – Performance measures need to be established. Without performance measures, how will a company know if the system is producing accurate reports? Performance measures can also help to analyze where problems are occurring. The problem may not be with the ERP system it could be with the company's business process or the user.

These are just a few of the characteristics associated with the TQM philosophy. There are others such as teamwork, total involvement of the company's people, and a continuing education training program. Companies want to successfully implement their ERP systems; but they also want to use it to manage the business and gain a competitive edge in the market place. Those who have been successful have continued to monitor their systems by applying TQM techniques to the ERP system.

4

Who is going to do it?

Most ERP implementations require a special team. This team is usually assembled from company employees and consultants. Each team member plays an important role. When roles and responsibilities are not clearly understood, problems soon arise. One of the most important roles is that of senior management. There are many different ways of organizing ERP teams, which make it difficult for companies to understand which method is best for their needs. Some ERP implementations take an enormous amount of employees' time learning how software works, talking with consultants, and setting up software and hardware.

In this chapter the reader will learn...

1. How does a company organize an ERP team?

2. What is the role of senior management?

3. What is the role of consultants and employees?

4. Who "owns" the ERP system?

5. What happens to the ERP team after implementation?

6. Who is "top management"?

Question: How does a company go about organizing its team for the implementation?

Ellen: The organization of the ERP implementation project team is crucial to a successful system implementation. There are many ways in which a company can organize the ERP team. The best organizational structure for an ERP team is the one that 'best' fits the company. Different positions on the team include: steering committee, executive sponsor, project manager, functional manager, team leader, team member, functional participant, application consultants, technical consultants, business consultants, IT members, and end users.

An ERP implementation project core team typically consists of 6 to 8 people devoted full-time to the project. Knowledgeable and experienced people should be chosen to make up the project core team. These individuals should have an in-depth working knowledge of the functional departments of the company. They should possess good communication skills, as the core team members will assist end users of the system. They will be instrumental in influencing others within the company to accept and take 'ownership' of the new ERP system.

The ERP project core team should be overseen by an executive steering committee. Senior management, key functional business associates, and members of the IT should be part of the core team group. CIBRES recommends that a project manager be assigned to manage the project. The project manager should be an internal company person – one who knows your business and the employees.

Consultants usually act as members of the ERP project core team. They may be application, technical, or business, consultants. The consultants' role is one of listening, advising, and supporting the project core team.

If a company had a project core team for selecting a system, these same team members can also serve on the implementation project team. It's important that the ERP team stay consistent before, during, and after implementation of the system.

Ronnie: Yes, Ellen and let me reiterate; the selection and organization of the implementation team is very critical to the success of any implementation project. Team members should possess good knowledge of the overall organization as well as good communication skills. The structure of the team may vary greatly from company to company. There is no "best for every situation" structure. The structure will depend on the situation at each company and the type of implementation methodology to be used.

Most implementation teams will consist of a steering committee, an executive sponsor or champion, a project manager, team leader, team members, functional manager or representative and functional team member, end users, and a representative from the service provider. In most implementations, a consultant is included as part of the project team.

Selection of the members of the project team should be based on their ability as opposed to their availability. Too often, individuals are selected to serve on the project team because they are or can be made available. The project team members must be able and willing to devote their time and support to the project for the implementation to be successful.

Question: What is the role of senior management?

Ronnie: Senior management serves as part of the steering committee to establish the vision and mission for the project. Senior managers provide high level strategy for the ERP system in relationship to other business objectives. Senior management must show their commitment to the project and provide motivational and inspirational support for the project, in addition to their financial support.

Ellen: Yes Ronnie, 100% commitment from senior management is absolutely essential for a successful ERP implementation project. Senior managers give the ERP project credibility and support. Top management establishes and communicates the company's visions for the 'new' ERP system. They are instrumental in letting everyone within the company know that the ERP implementation project is a number one priority for the company. This helps to make the ERP system 'real' to everyone within the company even before it is installed.

Without senior management commitment to the project, successful completion of the project is questionable.

Question: When we say that top management has to be involved, how is top management defined?

Ronnie: We define top management as the top level managers of the company. Ultimately, the overall responsibility for the success of the company lies with them. These individuals are the ultimate decision makers. Depending on the size of the company and the structure of the organization, these individuals may have a variety of titles.

Ellen: When companies implement an ERP system, members of the top management staff may view the ERP project and system as an IT project. They need to recognize that this is a business project because the system will affect the manner in which they run their business. They must be willing to support the ERP implementation project team. This support can take many forms: serving on the steering committee, filling the position of executive sponsor, or allocating resources to the project.

Top management helps establish the overall strategy for the ERP system as it relates to the company. They can establish vision and mission statements for the ERP system. They are a source of motivation and inspiration for the project.

Companies, who have had a high level of success with implementing ERP, say that top management involvement was a key critical success factor.

Question: What is the role of consultants?

Ellen: Consultants, first and foremost, should be listeners. If a consultant does not listen to the project core team, he or she can not understand what problems the team may be experiencing. Without having a full understanding of the problem, the consultant can not make any recommendations to solve the problem.

Beware

Beware of consultants that spend too much time talking. They will never understand you business if they do not listen.

There are 3 basic types of consultants that may be needed for an ERP implementation project: application, technical and management.

Application consultants focus on the software application. They are usually members of the ERP vendors' implementation staff. Education and training, demonstrating how the system works, and configuring the system are their primary concerns.

Management consultants focus on project management tasks. If a company does not have a person who can fill the position of project manager on the ERP core team, an outside management consultant may be hired for that role. Management consultants focus on the management of business process controls and procedures that need to be established. They often coordinate their efforts with the application consultant to make sure that both the system process and business process align with each other.

Technical consultants focus on the technical aspects of the project. They may be provided by the ERP vendor and assist in the installation of the ERP system. A company may hire outside technical consultants to configure servers, networks, EDI, or telecommunication equipment.

Regardless of the type of consultant a company may decide to use, consultants should not be allowed to 'take over' the project. Their roles and responsibilities should be clearly understood by everyone on the ERP project team. Good consultants listen to the ERP team members, understand the problems and make recommendations to solve the problems. Consultants can serve as troubleshooters by helping the team avoid possible looming problems. They can perform periodic quality assurance checks to make sure that the project is progressing as efficiently as possible.

A company can benefit from the professional services that consultants provide. How well the company benefits is dependent upon the consultants' professional skill level, their ability to listen, and their manner of delivering recommendations to the project team. The company must likewise be receptive to the consultants' recommendations and utilize their recommendations to help make the project a success.

Ronnie: Consultants also serve as a resource to assist in identifying problems and recommending solutions to the problems. As Ellen stated, it is the consultant's responsibilty to *listen* to the client. Consultants should *not* play the role of a decision maker. They should assist in providing the best possible potential solutions to the problems, but the final decision should remain the responsibility of the company management because the effects of the decisions being made will remain long after the consultant is gone.

Consultants may also serve in the role of a coach. In this role, they will assist company employees in understanding what is needed and required. Also, in this role, consultants may help in bringing out the potential in some of the employees.

Consultants also frequently perform the role of an auditor. Consultants can very effectively review your situation and progress toward resolution, and assist in keeping you on track.

Question: What is the role of middle managers?

Ellen: Middle managers usually fill the position of functional manager on the project team. This role fits the middle managers because they have oversight of the day to day operation of their departments. Middle managers are intimately familiar with the business processes of the company and how these processes relate to their functional area. This knowledge is an invaluable resource for configuring the system.

The functional manager needs to have conceptual skills in understanding the overall ERP project and how it relates to the functional areas of the business. The amount of time they spend on the project is usually minimal.

Ronnie: Middle managers represent their particular functions and provide the needed resources required from their respective areas. Their role, as with all management, is to demonstrate their support for the project.

Question: What is the role of general end users of an ERP system?

Ellen: End users of an ERP system include everyone in the company who will use the system. End user acceptance of the ERP system is critical and can make or break an ERP system.

            Unfortunately, many companies overlook the role of end users. Training programs, documentation, procedures, processes, and controls are often not explained to the end user. End users are often not informed about the project until the system is scheduled to 'go live'. When this occurs, many companies experience 'mutiny' on the part of the users. It is extremely important that companies recognize the importance of the end users and the role they have in connection with the ERP system.

            End users represent the largest group associated with an ERP system. Each user has his or her own skill set. Documentation and training programs need to be designed to specifically address the end users' concerns. For example, an accounts receivable clerk does not need to receive the same training as an accounts payable clerk.

Without end user acceptance, an ERP system may be successfully implemented, 'go-live', and then suffer a slow death.

Ronnie: End users also have the least control over the direction or the outcome of the project, but in most cases they are the most important part of the implementation. To be successful, the implementation requires a high acceptance level by the end user.

The importance of training the end users is too often overlooked or minimized. Obtaining input and feedback from the end users is also critical to the project's success.

Question: What is the role of the IS (Information Systems) department in an ERP system?

Ronnie: First, let's discuss what the role of the IS department is NOT. The IS department does not "own" the system. IS department employees are not users of the system so they really have no vested interest in the success of the project. The IS department is not responsible for deciding how a business should be run, they may be computer experts, but they are generally not business experts. IS is not responsible for the information provided by the system and they should not be responsible for selecting a software package.

So, then, what *is* the role of the IS department? The role the IS department has in an ERP system will vary from company to company, based upon the company structure, but the primary function of the Information Services department is to oversee the overall operations and maintenance of the computer systems. During implementation, IS should manage the technical aspects. Their role also includes providing programming, technical assistance including technical risk analysis, and application assistance when needed, if they have the expertise to do so.

Ellen: It is not unusual to go into a company and find that the ERP system was chosen by the IS department manager. The IS department configures the system according to what they think the company needs or wants. Unfortunately, the system rarely meets with acceptance from other members of management or the end users. Why? Because an ERP system is a business tool not an IS project.

An IS department is a valuable resource to a company. The IS department's role is primarily a technical role. This is especially 'true' when it comes to the ERP system. During the ERP implementation phase of the project, the IS department has a variety of tasks that they must complete. Designing the technical architecture needed for the ERP system, hardware equipment sizing, operating systems, telecommunication issues, EDI, program interfaces, data conversions, programming, and report writing are a few of the tasks associated with the IS department before, during, and after an ERP implementation.

After the ERP system goes 'live', the IS department is instrumental in keeping the network and operating system 'up' and 'running'. ERP system upgrades, interface maintenance, programming, system backup, and disaster recovery are all tasks that should be the responsibility of the IS department.

Companies need to recognize that the IS department is an organization's technical resource. As with any resource, companies that manage, educate, and value the IS resource have a greater chance of being successful with their ERP system.

Question: What are the role and responsibilities of a project manager?

Cibres

The *"ERP: A-Z Implementer's Guide for Success"* contains a detailed chapter on how form ERP teams. CIBRES item number 4516.

The project manager's role and responsibilities are directly 'tied' to how the ERP team was formed. Let's look at how the different ERP team strategies dictate the role and responsibilities of the project manager.

Isolated Functional Team Strategy – With this type of ERP team, functional managers are given the responsibility of implementing their functional areas of the system. There is no centralized resource coordinating or synchronizing of activities for implementing the ERP system. This type of team structure does not have a project manager. Unfortunately, this strategy should only be used by companies who have no competition from another company.

Lightweight Team Strategy – The lightweight team strategy would include functional managers, team lead persons, and a project manager. The project manager's role is one of providing support to the functional managers and lead persons. He or she is viewed more as a facilitator and communication channel.

Heavyweight Team Strategy – The project manager oversees the total project. It is his or her responsibility to communicate and coordinate the resources needed to complete the project on time and within budget. The project manager is usually the one who presides over the ERP core team meetings, issues resolutions, updates the executive sponsor and steering committee on the status of the ERP project, and prepares documentation relevant to the project. The heavyweight project manager has direct authority and control over the ERP core team.

In other words, the heavyweight project manager keeps a finger on the pulse of the ERP project, making sure that tasks are being completed on time. If tasks and deadlines are not being met, the project manager must make adjustments to address these issues quickly; otherwise, the project can become stagnant, go over budget, and not be successfully completed.

A-Team Strategy – This team strategy demands a heavyweight powerful project manager. While the project manager's role and responsibility contains all the same characteristics as the heavyweight approach, roles and responsibilities of the ERP core team members can fluctuate and change as the situation and project manager dictates.

A project manager's role in an ERP project can be a 'tough' job. Senior management often looks to the project manager to make sure that the ERP project stays on time, within budget, and is successful. Every project manager hopes to accomplish a successful ERP project. That is a project manager's reward for a job well done!

Ronnie: The role and responsibilities of the project manager vary depending on what type of project team is formed. Regardless of the type of project team, project managers should possess good communication skills, leadership skills, and management skills. Project managers may be selected from within the organization or an outside source may be chosen to serve as project manager.

The project manager must be able to exert authority and influence to persuade others in achieving the project goals. A good project manager encourages team work while recognizing individuals for their efforts. A good project manager must be willing to accept blame, listen to other team members, and to communicate the vision to others.

Question: How do we know if our company needs a project manager?

Ronnie: Most implementations need a project manager, even though "project manager" may not be their official title. To determine if your company needs a project manager, review the performance and effectiveness of past projects. Have past projects had a project manager? If not, how successful were they? If yes, how successful were those projects? How large is this project? Most importantly, how important is the success of this project to the success of your company? After answering these questions, most companies will realize they have a definite need for a project manager.

Ellen: It is true that any successful project requires a project plan and people to execute that plan. This is never truer than when a company is embarking on an ERP implementation project. Assigning a project manager to an ERP project is a 'best practice' recommendation.

The project manager should possess project management skills and be an internal person who is familiar with the company's business. He or she may have already assisted another company with a similar ERP implementation. The project manager should be familiar with the problems that the ERP core team may encounter as the ERP project progresses. If the company can not find an appropriate person from within, there are many reputable external sources where a company can find a skilled project manager.

The project manager acts as a facilitator to the core team members – helping them to resolve issues as they crop up during the project. The project manager keeps management informed as to the project status, thereby keeping senior management involved with the project.

Every company must decide whether they want or need a project manager. ERP projects that include a skilled project manager usually complete on time, within budget, and successfully.

Question: What happens to the team after the implementation is complete?

Ronnie: In most instances, the project team is dismantled and members return to the duties they performed prior to becoming a member of the project team. In some cases, some of the members are recognized for their efforts on the project and are assigned to other projects or they are promoted. Some team members leave the company because the excitement of the challenge no longer exists. But, the idea that the project has ended and the implementation is complete can be very misleading.

Ellen: You are right, Ronnie, and it is also important to recognize that ERP project teams can provide continuous ongoing support and maintenance of the ERP system after the implementation is completed. Members of the team represent the people who have the inside knowledge about the system. They helped to install, configure, and implement the system. They played a key role in developing processes, procedures and controls for the system. They probably were also instrumental in the training and education of end users of the system.

             While some of the team members will return to their functional area full-time, others may act as advisors within their functional area on system questions or issues. They may still attend periodic meetings to discuss issues or concerns regarding the system.

The completion of the implementation should not be viewed as the ending of the project; rather it is the beginning of the next phase of the project.

Question: Who has the most responsibility for ensuring the success of an ERP system?

Ellen: ERP is a people system. That means that no one person or department within an organization is responsible for its success or failure.

A successful ERP project requires commitment, support, cooperation and acceptance from senior management to the person running the press on the production floor. Senior management 'sets' the company attitude toward the ERP system by communicating to everyone that they are 100% committed to the success of the ERP system. Department managers and users of the system adhere to the company's controls, procedures and processes for conducting daily business. Standards for data collection and data entry into the system are followed by the person on the shop floor to the data entry clerk; thereby, helping to maintain data integrity within the ERP system.

Responsibility for ensuring the success of an ERP system lies squarely on the people who use, maintain, and support the system. The people within a company must take 'ownership' of the system. It is their business tool to manage and maintain.

Ronnie: Yes, and consultants may also play a role in the project, but the project and responsibility for its success really belong to the company. Vendors are often blamed for the failure of an implementation or failure of the system to perform, but if the vendor provides a working software and the services agreed upon, the vendor has fulfilled its responsibility. It should be remembered, this is not an IS project, it is a company-wide project. Too often, the IS department is recognized as having responsibility for ensuring that the company has a successful implementation and is used as a scapegoat when the implementation fails or the results are far from what was expected.

Top management must be commited to the project and supply adequate resources. The steering committee must give direction. The software vendor must provide the software and services agreed upon. The consultants must provide assistance and guidance. The project team must establish a plan and execute it. But, ultimately, the end users must take ownership of the ERP system and make it successful.

Question: What are responsibilities of the ERP vendor?

Ellen: The responsibility of the ERP vendor begins and ends with the customer. During the ERP system selection process the ERP vendor is contacted for information relating to their products and services. The ERP vendor may give a scheduled demonstration of their products. As with any company that sells and services products, the ERP vendor is interested in making a 'sale'; therefore, the vendor will consistently 'court' the prospective customer.

After viewing the demonstrated ERP solution, the customer requests a business proposal (quotation) from the vendor. The ERP business proposal usually contains the following:

Executive Summary – The executive summary is comprised of 2 parts: (1) an executive overview and (2) a proposed solution overview. This contains information relating to the vendor's perception and understanding as to the customer's objectives. It gives reasons why the ERP vendor feels that their solution will meet the needs of the customer.

Proposed Solution – This section gives a detailed overview of the proposed ERP solution. It covers technology requirements, ERP solution transactional description, system tools and utilities, workflow automation capabilities, and optional modules. These optional modules usually pertain to areas of concern that lie outside the core package such as bar coding, e-business, facility maintenance, etc.

ERP Vendor – This contains the ERP vendor's history, company vision, business philosophy, and an overview of the company and the ERP software. It is within this section that the ERP vendor outlines services that they offer such as maintenance, on-going support, training, and system documentation. It is also within this section of the proposal that special conditions may be found. Many vendors will add disclaimers to the proposal. These disclaimers are a means that vendors have to protect themselves against unrealistic customer expectations.

Investment Summary – This section contains all pricing information regarding the proposed ERP solution as well as proposed services. Training, installation, maintenance, on-going support, and system upgrades are detailed and priced for the customer. Terms and conditions are also outlined in this section. If the customer decides to purchase the ERP software, agreements relating to the sale of the software and services are also included at the end of the business proposal.

Some companies do not want any of the ERP vendor's services. They want only to purchase the software solution. In this case, the ERP vendor's responsibility is to deliver the ERP solution and documentation to the customer in excellent condition. If, during the installation of the software, it is discovered that a CD is defective, the ERP vendor has the responsibility to replace the defective CD.

The extent of the ERP vendor's responsibilities lies primarily with the customer's decision-makers. The company dictates where the ERP vendor responsibility will begin and where it ends.

Ronnie: And may I add, the software vendor's responsibility is to provide the software and services as agreed upon. The vendor should be honest and forthcoming as in all business dealings, but that is not always the case. Remember, the vendor wants to make a sale. The customer should be aware that the vendor has very little responsibility for the success of the project. That responsibility lies within the company itself.

Responsibilities of the vendor may vary based upon the items that are agreed upon during negotiations. Most vendors offer services to assist in the implementation of the software and in user training, including providing consulting. The extent of these services should be carefully documented during the negotiation phase prior to the signing of any agreement. Obtain a clarification of what is considered consulting time. How many calls or how many hours of time does the vendor agree to offer before additional costs are incurred? Most items are negotiable; just be careful to have clear, precise documentation of the responsibilities that the vendor agreed upon.

Question: Who should really "own" the system?

Ronnie: The end users should own the system. It is their system. They use it to perform their job functions. They should bear the responsibility of the ownership of the system.

Ellen: Ronnie, I would say a company's ERP system is 'owned' by the people within the organization. It is *their* system that must be managed, maintained and supported. An ERP system suffering from a lack of user ownership will never perform or live up to the expectations of senior management. The data will not be reliable; thereby making the reports that are needed to make financial decisions, be inaccurate. In time, the ERP system will fail.

Lack of ownership sends a 'red' flag that the ERP system is in trouble.

A successful ERP system requires commitment, support, cooperation, and acceptance, from senior management to the person running the press on the production floor. Senior management 'sets' the company attitude toward the ERP system by communicating to everyone that they are 100% committed to the success of the ERP system. Department managers and users of the system adhere to the company's controls, procedures, and processes for conducting daily business. Standards for data collection and data entry into the system are followed by the person on the shop floor to the data entry clerk; thereby, helping to maintain data integrity within the ERP system.

Many companies make the error of turning ownership of the ERP system over to the IS department. This often leads to disputes between members of the IS department and the users of the system - each side blaming the other when ERP system problems occur. The ERP system soon becomes an IMS (information management system). It's seen as a very expensive data collection and storage tool. The quality and maintenance of the data is not controlled. As a result, in time, the ERP system will be of little or no use to the company.

The ownership of an ERP system lies squarely on the people who use, maintain, and support the system. The people within a company must take 'ownership' of the system. It is their business tool to manage and maintain.

5

How is it going to happen?

Choosing what ERP system to use can be a daunting task. There are over 1000 ERP vendors on the market providing all types of unique solutions using different technologies for specific industries. After the purchase of an ERP system many companies become uncertain what their next step should be. And when things do not go well, they become even more uncertain. Often priorities and the focus of resources are misappropriated. Education and training play key roles throughout the life of an ERP system. The length of an ERP implementation can range from a few months to many years. For many companies, implementation becomes a continuous process throughout the life of their ERP system.

In this chapter the reader will learn ...

1. How does a company choose an ERP system?

2. How is the transition performed?

3. What happens after implementation?

4. How long will it take?

5. Why do companies not invest in ERP education?

6. What are different methods for Installing ERP?

Question: I have read that there are over 1000 ERP vendors providing different types of software solutions. How does a company like mine choose the right ERP vendor?

Ronnie: In my opinion, selecting the correct ERP vendor and software is the second most important step of the implementation, second only to the decision to do an implementation. Therefore, it is something that your company should not take lightly. During the implementation project planning stages, you should perform a needs analysis. The needs analysis identifies what the company needs from an ERP system. During the process of performing the needs analysis you must consider the long term business objectives, direction of the business, and growth potential.

    The Business Integration Planning session combines the information gathered from the needs analysis with the operational requirements to meet future business objectives. This integrated business plan provides the basis for the ERP system requirements.

    Next, prepare Request for Information (RFI) packets and send them to potential ERP vendors who were identified. You can find potential ERP vendors or service providers by gathering information from the Internet, trade magazines, through acquaintances, advertisements, etc. The RFI is a request for general information about the vendor and the product. How much does the product cost? How many functional modules are available? What is the vendor's market share? These are just a few of the general questions your company should ask. The RFIs are really just an information gathering exercise. Along with the RFIs, begin the general research of potential vendors.

After reviewing the RFIs, narrow down the potential vendors. Then send a Request for Proposal (RFP) or Request for Quote (RFQ) to the potential vendor. The RFP contains questions designed to determine if the ERP vendor's product will provide the business functionality necessary to meet the needs of your company. Base the RFP on the information obtained from the needs analysis and the integrated business plan. Once the RFPs are received, review them and narrow down the potential candidates even further. Along with RFPs, check references; conduct reference site surveys. ERP vendors should conduct a site survey to learn more about your company, how it operates, and what its needs are.

Formulate a Demo Script to provide a documented standard demonstration method for each of the ERP vendors to follow. CIBRES recommends that you require all potential ERP vendors to follow the same demo script. Following the demo scripts, a software demo should be provided to allow the critical stakeholders an opportunity to view the product. During the software demo, encourage individuals to ask questions and express any concerns they may have. There are several types of software demos, some being of very little use while others provide a real opportunity to see how the software performs. Some vendors prefer to use a canned or preloaded package to show what is available with their software. CIBRES recommends having the demo use data provided by your company and performing the functions required to meet your company's needs.

After the demos, after all the information gathering, after all the discussions of the pros and cons of the various softwares, it is time to make a decision. This is one of the most critical business decisions that your company will make and this decision will have a long lasting effect on your company. Once your company makes the decision to commit to one software, it is very difficult to change the decision and go a different direction. The decision making should involve your company's critical stakeholders. The decision to use a particular software must have the support of all the stakeholders. That does not mean that it must be a unanimous decision, only that each participant will support the decision.

Ellen: You know, Ronnie, several years ago when a company decided to select an ERP system, they found that their choices were limited. Now that has changed. The choices available to companies can be overwhelming. Care must be taken because choosing the wrong ERP solution could mean disaster for a company.

The Internet can prove to be a valuable tool to any company searching for information on possible ERP vendors. ERP vendors usually have their own websites where prospective customers can read about them, their solutions, and services. The CIBRES organization website has an ERP vendor chart where they maintain ERP vendor information such as size of the company, which industries they serve, types of environment (discrete, process, hybrid), and links to the vendor's website.

You should approach the task of choosing an ERP system as you would an ERP project. As with any project, planning is important for its successful completion. There are several tasks that you need to address prior to contacting any ERP vendor. Your company must first define what critical criteria the proposed system must be able to meet. These criteria would be a combination of current and future business process needs. You should base the needs upon information supplied to the ERP project core team by management, users, and other sources. Send this information to prospective vendors in the form of an RFP. This is usually the first contact a company would have with a prospective ERP vendor.

ERP vendors usually respond very quickly to an RFP. To the vendor, the RFP represents a possible 'sale' of their ERP solution as well as future long-term services. To the company looking for an ERP solution, the RFP is a means that they can narrow down the ERP vendor choices to the top 3 or 4 vendors. Contact the top ERP vendors to schedule a demonstration of their software solution. This initial demonstration can give your company a chance to get an overview of the software and meet and talk 'face-to-face' with the vendor. Your company may narrow down the choices to one or two vendors. Invite these top vendors back for a very extensive 2 or 3 day presentation of their solution. This presentation should be presented not only to core team members but key users of the system. It is important that during these presentations the core team members and users 'drive' the demonstration – not the vendor. Upon completion of these demonstrations, the ERP system selection core team will be in a better position to choose an ERP vendor that can provide your company with an ERP system that meets your company's critical system needs.

Choosing an ERP vendor can seem like an impossible task – so many vendors and solutions. Following a system selection methodology can help your company narrow down the list of vendors that you need to contact. There are many reputable consulting firms that specialize in helping companies during this process. A company should not select an ERP vendor or ERP solution based on an advertisement, magazine article, or casual conversation with another manager.

Question: How do companies go about choosing an ERP system?

Ellen: CIBRES recommends that when your company decides to implement an ERP system, you follow a formal system selection process. Many outside consulting companies, such as the CIBRES Organization, PricewaterhouseCoopers, or Deloitte &Touché, have developed system selection methodologies that help to ensure that a company chooses the best possible ERP solution. The system selection methodology followed by reputable organizations provides companies with the needed knowledge to make the best choice for their company.

The system selection process contains several key factors that help to make the choice a successful one. Some of these are:

Planning – Planning can not be overemphasized. Planning is a key success factor. Many of the activities undertaken during the system selection process will 'carry over' into the implementation phase.

Project Team – As with any project, you should form a project team. This team should contain not only management staff but should extend out to the users of the system. While users may not actually sit in on the core team meetings, their input is critical to the success of the project. No one knows their jobs better than the end users. They can bring to the project tips on the daily activities that many within the organization are not aware of. Team members who share in the system selection phase usually serve on the ERP implementation core team.

Project Team Members – Choose the project team members carefully. This is in part because any ERP project is considered to be complicated. Many factors such as technology, complexity, and diversity of the project require skilled people to serve on the team. Choose individuals who not only possess the needed skills to complete the tasks but also people who have a thorough working knowledge of the business. It is one thing to know how a business process should function; but it is another to have actual working experience of that process.

Project Leader or Management – It is important to head the project with someone who has the authority to make decisions quickly. He or she should have good communication skills and be recognized as a leader for the team. They need to understand the why, where, when, and how of the project. Management needs to communicate to others within the company that the project leader/manager has their full support and the authority of 'take charge' of the project. Without this, the project will not be successful.

System Selection Process Methodology – A project needs to be completed within budget, on time, and successfully. You need to determine the project scope, budgetary concerns, timelines, and tasks. You can address all of these issues by using and following a system selection process methodology. Define the roles and responsibilities for the team members. Assign tasks. Calculate and note dates for completion of those tasks. Failure to follow a structured project methodology may result in the project going over budget, missing deadlines, and most disastrous, choosing the wrong ERP solution.

Define Critical System Criteria – It is critical that your company looks at their current business process, future business and technology plans, and critical requirements for the system. For example, all ERP systems have production modules. One of the areas that usually causes a problem with these systems is the way the system handles sub-contracting for outside processing of an item. If sub-contracting is a daily activity for your production, you need to investigate this thoroughly. During the vendor demonstration, the core team members would want to make sure the vendor not only 'says' that the software can do sub-contracting but demonstrates it.

These are examples of some of the key areas that your company should address during a system selection project. Many times ERP systems are chosen as a matter of the CEO having a conversation out on the golf course with a friend or associate. Unfortunately, this often has very bad results for the company that purchases an ERP solution based on this type of information.

Ronnie: As I previously stated, the steps for selecting the best software to match your company's needs are:

1. Needs analysis,
2. Business integration planning,
3. RFIs,
4. RFPs,
5. Demo scripts,
6. Software demonstrations, and
7. Site and reference surveys.

However, software is only a part of the ERP system, a tool to be used. There is no "canned" ERP system. Prior to software selection, prior to the needs analysis and business integration planning, your company management team must evaluate the:

- Business objectives,
- Business plan,
- Goals, and
- Company vision.

From this evaluation, a set of operating policies, principles, and procedures are established.

These principles, policies, procedures, along with the vision for your company should guide you while selecting the software to be used and the people that will use the software. Many companies choose to utilize outside help such as the CIBRES organization, Price-Waterhouse-Coopers, etc. to assist in selection.

You should not select the software without proper planning and evaluation. You must define criteria critical to your organization. You should follow a well defined software selection process.

Question: Is an ERP system designed to fit a certain business environment, such as automotive, or do good ERP systems adapt to any business environment?

Ellen: ERP systems do not come in a 'one size fits all' package. ERP solutions vary in their flexibility and adaptability to different industrial environments. There are ERP solutions that are specifically designed to 'fit' the needs of the retail industry, such as grocery stores. A process manufacturer needs an ERP system that addresses their inventory and production needs. Process manufacturers have recipes rather than structured bills of material. Raw materials may be purchased in pounds, stored in ounces, and used in the recipe as kilograms.

Some ERP vendors have combined traditional ERP functionality with vertical-market needs to create a single integrated solution. For example, one popular ERP vendor combines many of the traditional ERP solutions designed for discrete manufacturers into a vertical market application for the helicopter industry.

It is important for companies to remember that the best ERP system is the ERP solution that meets at least 95% of their company's critical criteria.

Ronnie: As Ellen stated, different ERP systems work better in different business environments. Different types of industries have different requirements and needs and the software is programmed to meet those standards. For example, a software package designed to function very well in a flow manufacturing environment might not work as well in a batch or process manufacturing environment. However, the major software packages can be adapted to work in most any environment. It is very uncommon for any canned software package to provide the exact functionality a company needs. Most implementations will require either some modifications to the software or a change in the methods used to run the business.

The software selected should mirror the company's defined business "best practices" and work flows as closely as possible and should meet the critical criteria that was defined for the software. Normally, canned software packages require some modifications; but, as Ellen stated, the software package as purchased should fulfill at least 95% of the criteria.

Question: After we start an implementation what can we expect to happen?

Ellen: After months of anticipation the big day arrives. Implementation of the new ERP system begins. The implementation of an ERP system can evoke a series of different reactions from people within the organization. These reactions can range from excitement of working with a new, improved ERP system to fear of the 'unknown'. These reactions are why change management is so important to the success of an ERP implementation.

The changes that will occur within an organization during the implementation of an ERP system can be compared to a bell-shaped graph.

At the onset of the implementation process, everyone within the organization must face the realization that this 'new' ERP system is going to be implemented, go 'live' and soon replace their old way of doing their jobs. The implementation will mean they have to learn a 'new' system, adapt to new business processes, and possibly be reassigned to another job position. During this stage, confusion and anxiety will increase. If the organization does not have a means to manage this reaction, the successful completion of the ERP implementation could be jeopardized.

Confidence within the organization also follows this same bell-shaped graph. In the beginning, there is usually a high degree of confidence towards a 'new' ERP system. As the workload increases and the complexity of the project is realized, confidence can rapidly deteriorate. Problems with hardware, software, lack of ownership, and lack of knowledge will gradually diminish individual confidence in the 'new' ERP system. The confidence level within the organization will remain unstable throughout the project until the system is 'live', processes are in place, and people have been trained. Once people realize that this 'new' ERP system will work, confidence levels within the organization will start to rise.

An ERP system represents change. It can not be stressed enough that any company that is implementing an ERP system must include change management in the project plan. Many ERP implementations have failed due to the organization not planning for change.

Ronnie: That's right, Ellen, change management is very important to the success of the project. Resistance to change needs to be addressed. Individuals must be "coached" to accept the changes they will experience with the coming of a new system.

Confidence in a new system must be won. The new system is replacing a system that people were both familiar and comfortable with. This implementation is taking away their security blanket. The fear of the unknown will often cause stress and tension.

During this time period, good communications are most important, communications of what to expect, what progress has been made, and what effect, if any, the new system will have on the individuals and the way they perform their jobs. Good open communications will eliminate much of the resistance to change.

Question: How will we make the transition from our old ERP system to our new one?

Ellen:

Cibres

The *"ERP: A-Z Implementer's Guide for Success"* contains a detailed chapter on different transition methods in an ERP implementation. CIBRES item number 4516.

Making the transition from old to new appears to be a simple procedure. Often many people assume that the transition should be minor; however, this is seldom the case. The transition strategy determines how the new ERP system will be implemented. Implementing an ERP system is a complex process. Companies should give special attention to the transitional plan for the new system.

There are several basic ERP transition strategies. Lets examine the pros and cons associated with each of these strategies.

Big Bang Strategy – This strategy is considered to be the most difficult and aggressive approach. A company decides on a 'go-live' date, turns off the legacy system, and turns on the new system. The entire enterprise is converted to the new ERP system simultaneously.

Many companies elect not to use this strategy. It is not the recommended method for a company to transfer to a new ERP system because of the number of resources required to support the go live of the ERP system. Everyone within the organization must cooperate and accept the new system at the same time. This is difficult because everyone's skill level with the new system is different.

For the big bang strategy to be successful, a company must invest a lot of time and money into planning for the go live of the system.

Phased Strategy – This is the most common approach. The phased approach implements one module at a time. The financial module is usually the first module to be implemented. This is a key module because of the general ledger links to the other modules such as distribution and production. One of the advantages to this strategy is that many companies feel more comfortable phasing in a new system. As they become more familiar with the system, their comfort level with the system increases. Another advantage is that there is less risk with this strategy. Failure of one functional module is easier to deal with than an enterprise-wide system failure.

A disadvantage to this approach is the technical resource requirement. Maintaining two ERP systems, interfacing the systems, and data conversions are tasks that require technical expertise. This can put an added 'stress' on an already overloaded IT department. A phased approach usually requires more time and overall cost to implement the system. Key people on the ERP team come and go due to the length of the project.

Parallel Strategy – The parallel approach does not turn off the legacy system until the company feels comfortable with the new system. Both systems are run simultaneously. One of the advantages to this approach is less risk. If something goes wrong with the new system, the company can continue to operate while the new system is corrected. This approach also allows users to become comfortable with the new system before losing their legacy system.

A disadvantage is that transactions must be duplicated. Data must be entered and processed in the legacy system. The same data has to be entered and processed in the new system. This doubles the workload of the users.

This approach works well for mission critical situations that cannot afford a malfunction. It also works well for organizations that require a stable 24/7-system operation.

I have addressed three examples of transition strategies that a company may elect to use for implementing their new ERP system. Each company must decide for themselves which transition strategy fits their particular organization. It is important that each company not only counts the 'cost' of each transitional strategy, but also takes into account their organizational culture – the people.

Ronnie: There are several ERP transition strategies that may be utilized. These methods are the big bang or cold turkey method, parallel, and phased, which

Ellen discussed. There are also the process, and hybrid methods, which I will discuss shortly.

Transition from the old system to the new system is more than just converting the data from the old system to the new system. Transitioning from the old system to the new system also includes new methods and ways of doing business.

To make the transition, regardless of the strategy used, data must be converted. To convert the data, electronic conversion or manual input of data may be used. Which of these two methods is best? It all depends on the situation at the particular company, the time allotted to do the conversion, and the resources available for conversion. Both methods of conversion have their pros and cons.

The electronic conversion of data is fast. Generally, the electronic conversion provides accurate migration of information from one system to another. The down side to this method is the information is converted as it is; if it is inaccurate, then inaccurate information is moved into the new system. Electronic conversion may require some programming costs to allow a bridge to be established between the old and new systems.

Manual conversion is usually slower than electronic conversion. Additional or temporary help is required to perform the data input or to perform other tasks while regular employees perform the data input. One benefit of manual conversion is the data can be checked for accuracy as it is being input. Another, and maybe the #1 benefit of this method, is this is an excellent training tool for the users. The repetition of performing the inputs into the system prepares the end users to perform their jobs, and increases their confidence and acceptance of the system.

Each of the methods for transitioning from the legacy system to the new system has its advantages and disadvantages. The Big Bang/ Cold Turkey approach is generally not recommended. Normally this approach requires more resources to support the "go live". However, it can save money because there is no need for interface programs between the legacy system and the new system since all modules are implemented at the same time. If organized properly, this approach can be just as successful as any other approach.

The Phased approach normally takes longer because modules are implemented at different times so the complete cut over from old to new is extended.

The Parallel approach consists of running the old and the new systems at the same time. This is the preferred method by many companies. The company continues with the old system until they are comfortable with the new. This requires double the data input, increases the probability of error, and can cause considerable amount of work trying to resolve issues when the systems become out of sync. Which system contains the correct information? Both have to be reviewed. Another approach to parallel is to do a "paper parallel", which eliminates entries into the old system but still provides a little feeling of security.

The Process line approach may work best for some companies if there are distinctly differing process lines such as a manufacturer that may have a line to produce washers and a line to produce dryers. It is not suited well for most companies. Using the process line strategy, after the washer line successfully completes the transition, the dryer line begins the trasistion from the legacy system to the new one.

The hybrid strategy is another method that may be utilized. The hybrid strategy may consist of any combination of the phased, parallel, and process strategies. This strategy usually evolves over the life of the project as team members learn more about the software, business processes and procedures, and as the scope of the project changes. An advantage of using this strategy is the flexibility it provides in adapting to the needs of the organization as differing situations arise. A disadvantage to this approach is that it can become difficult for the team to adjust. Good communication is required regardless of the transition method chosen, but, because of the nature of the strategy, the hybrid approach relies on communication and strong, effective leadership more than any of the other approaches.

Question: What are the different ways of implementing an ERP system?

Ellen: There are various methods available for implementing an ERP system. ERP vendors have their own preferred implementation strategy.

Leading ERP professionals have their opinions on which strategy works better.

Implementing an ERP system is a complex process. Implementation strategies have advantages and disadvantages associated with them. One is not necessarily better than another one. Each company must decide which implementation strategy best 'fits' their organizational structure and culture. Let's discuss some of the leading strategies for implementing an ERP system.

Break Neck Strategy – On the surface, this strategy appears to require less resources for the implementation. It requires little planning and lower initial cost; however, it's considered to be the most risky because a number of important tasks are eliminated. Most companies who elect to use this strategy find that they encounter more problems. Some of these problems are configuration, performance, functional and organizational issues. This strategy usually results in a tremendous amount of work to 'fix' the problems associated with a 'speedy' implementation.

Budget Strategy – The budget strategy is very similar to the break neck strategy. The company sets the project budget. Implementation costs must stay within the confines of the budget. One of the problems with this type of strategy is that a company usually underestimates the total cost of the project.

Low Risk Strategy – This strategy consists of a detailed project plan listing all of the tasks needed for a successful implementation. During the course of the implementation, audits are conducted to make sure that none of the steps are being skipped and deadlines are being met. Some of the advantages to this strategy are maximum benefits with minimal business disruptions. Disadvantages include lengthy implementation time, dedicated full time resources, and increased cost.

Turnkey Strategy – The ERP implementation is outsourced. The company has little or no input as to how the system is planned or implemented. This represents a high risk to most companies because no one knows your business better than your company's own internal staff and management. The only advantage to this type of strategy is that it requires no or little company internal resources. The disadvantages are cost, lack of ownership, missing functionality, and vendor turnover vulnerability.

ERP implementations are complex projects. A company must decide which implementation methodology will give their company the greatest chance for a successful implementation. When considering which implementation strategy to use, the people, processes, and technology that support the system need to be figured into the 'equation'. Without even one of these supporting pieces, the ERP implementation can disintegrate and fail.

Ronnie: Ellen, if you ask me; there are really only 2 ways of implementing an ERP system, the correct way (successful) or the wrong way (failure). However, different methods and approaches to implementation include: break neck, turnkey, in-house, budget, partner, low risk, and star. Ellen, you addressed the break-neck, budget, low risk, and turnkey strategies, so I'll address the in-house, star, and partner approaches.

The in-house approach utilizes internal resources as much as possible. While this approach builds internal ownership, it can cause long implementation times, and usually results in the company receiving less than full benefits from the system.

The partner approach is a combination of resources from inside the company and external resources such as consultants and service providers. The responsibilities for success are shared between the internal and external resources. When the desired results are not achieved, animosity and finger pointing develops between the groups. This partnering of responsibilities increases the chance for failure.

The star approach combines positive characteristics of the other methods. This approach can be described as the low risk approach with emphasis on implementation speed or the partner approach having responsibility for success remaining internally.

Regardless of which method a company selects, successful (correct way) implementation projects normally have a great deal in common. They have top management support, a well selected and trained project team, and a well developed project plan, including timeline, tasks, responsibilities, deadlines, and accountability.

Question: How much time will it take to install an ERP system at our company?

Ronnie: The length of time to install an ERP system will vary from company to company. Two key factors that influence the time required are the size and complexity of the software being implemented and the method of implementation used. Implementations may range from as short as 6 months to as long as several years. An average implementation is approximately 18 months from beginning education to "go live".

The longer the implementation, generally the more costly the implementation and the greater chance of failure. Poor project planning and "project scope creep" both will increase the implementation time required.

There are two approaches that can be used to determine how long the project will take. One approach is to set a "go live" date and work everything backwards (backscheduling) and comprise the tasks and timelines to meet this "drop dead" date. This approach is usually dictated by top management. The second approach uses forward scheduling. The project plan and timeline is broken down into tasks, the length of time for task completion is calculated, and the timeline grows to the end or "go live" date. This method is the normal, most successful method, but caution must be taken not to pad the timeline too much and drag the project. Lengthy implementations have a way of failing.

Ellen: Yes, Ronnie, there is no hard and fast rule as to the amount of time it will take to implement an ERP system. With careful planning you can develop a projected timeline for assigning completion dates to implementation tasks.

The formula used to calculate the total project time for an ERP implementation is simple. Project time equals total calculated workdays divided by the total calculated full-time employees. This formula should be applied to every phase of the project. The figures are then totaled to get an overall project time.

Although this formula is easy and simple for calculating total project time, it is a fact that most companies vastly underestimate the time required to complete an ERP implementation project. That is because the scope of the project and resources are directly linked to the amount of time required for the project. If a project begins to experience "project scope creep", you must increase the time required for the project. If the required resources, such as people to perform the work, are not available, you must increase the project time.

Question: Why do most companies fail to invest in basic education for ERP systems?

Ellen: The reason why most companies fail to invest in basic education for ERP systems is that they often view ERP in much the same way as they view a software package like Microsoft Word. An ERP system is looked upon as just another piece of software. It is often thought to be an IT project.

Senior management assumes that the IT department knows how to implement an ERP system since they have installed other software. Management does not understand that when an ERP system is an enterprise-wide solution, it affects the very core of how their business functions.

There are many misconceptions about ERP. It is important that individuals understand what ERP really is, its impact on the business, how to manage the ERP implementation project, how to avoid disastrous project 'pitfalls', and how to maintain the ERP system after the 'go live' date. The CIBRES organization offers ERP educational seminars, material, and certifications to individuals. A visitor to their website can register for seminars, order educational materials, and chat online with certified professionals. There is even an online ERP question and answer wizard for individuals to access.

Basic ERP education and training must be conducted as an integral part of the ERP project, and the earlier the knowledge transfer occurs in the implementation process, the better the chances for successful ERP adoption

Ronnie: Ellen, this reminds me of a quote by Derek Bok, "If you think education is expensive, try ignorance." Most companies do not recognize the need to educate their employees on the basic concepts of ERP. As a matter of practice, most companies fail to recognize the need for continued education of any kind for most of the workforce. It is fairly common for companies to fail to provide sufficient training for their employees. In general, management does a poor job of realizing that employees are more valuable if they have the "know why" something is done as well as the "know how".

Most companies fail to understand the difference in training and education. The idea exists that if employees are trained to perform a function well enough to do their job, then there is no need to educate them to understand why they perform the function in that particular way.

In many companies top management doesn't really understand what ERP is or how large an undertaking an ERP implementation is. As Ellen stated, they view ERP as just software that should not be too difficult to learn to use. This misconception and lack of understanding on their part is reflected in their attitude toward education and training needs for the organization.

Question: Is it better for companies to do in-house training or should they send people to outside classes?

Ronnie: First let's distinguish the difference between education and training. Education is learning the "why" while training is learning the "how". The decision to do either education or training in-house versus sending the people outside depends upon the company, the employees' current aptitude, the type of training, and the number of participants to attend. It is usually more cost efficient to provide education or training in-house if there will be a large number of particpants. If only a few are to attend, depending on location, and type of training, it is often more cost efficient to have the classes conducted outside.

When classes are conducted outside, it generally requires travel and takes the employee away from their normal job duties for a longer period of time than in-house classes. But that can also be an advantage because, all too often, if the classes are conducted in-house, the employees have a tendency to try to perform some of their normal duties and do not devote their full attention to the classes being conducted.

The train-the-trainer concept is a commonly used approach to training. One or two individuals go off-site to receive in-depth training and then they train other users in-house. An advantage to using this type of training is that these trainers usually become experts in various functions or modules. These trainers are available to train new employees after the implementation is complete and may be utilized for help desk support.

In-house versus outside, all depends on the company culture and employees' needs. Each company must decide what is best for their situation. What works best for one company does not always work best for another. In-house training for large groups may be best, outside for a limited number of individuals.

Ellen: There is no doubt that when a company implements an ERP system that training is an important issue. The environment in which the training is conducted should be a primary concern. Many ERP vendors offer a variety of training options to companies, including web classes, on-site training, and off-site classes. A company should evaluate which of these options 'fits' their business environment and people better. In which setting would their people derive the most benefit?

Most companies elect not to use the web classes initially. It is felt that for initial training and education on the ERP system it is important that a 'live' trainer be available not only to answer questions but also to demonstrate the process flow for the group. Having this one-on-one interaction, people tend to retain the information better than attending a web class.

In-house training has its advantages. The ERP trainer comes on-site to teach the group. The class can be structured around the company's system needs. The group is free to ask questions regarding their specific functional areas. If the trainer does not have an answer for them immediately, he or she can request the information and get back with the group later in the training. There is usually time for members of the group to work one-on-one with the trainer either on the system or resolving issues.

In-house training is usually more appealing to companies but there must be 'ground rules' established for the training. For example, I attended the in-house training sessions held at two different companies as an observer. Let's look at what transpired during these training sessions.

Company A prepared a fully equipped classroom. Class rosters were prepared so everyone knew where and when they needed to be in class. The roster was then given to the receptionist and others within the organization with instructions that the people would not be available during those times. They were not to receive telephone calls, pages, or taken out of class unless it was a dire emergency. Having the classroom prepared, 'ground rules' established, and the groups prepared ahead of time, this in-house training proved to be very successful.

Company B also prepared a classroom. At the ERP vendor's expense, laptop computers with the training system installed, plus the server, had been shipped to the company two weeks prior to the trainer arriving at the facility. The company had agreed that they would set up the systems, ready the room, arrange their peoples' work schedules so that the classes could commence promptly on the scheduled date and time. The trainer arrived at the company prepared to begin the class; however, neither the room nor the equipment had been set up. No one knew who was to be in attendance or which session they were to attend. The trainer and I took 4 hours getting the room and equipment ready. She notified the project manager that the people needed to be in class promptly at 1:00 PM. He agreed. At 1:00 PM the trainer was ready but only one person was there – me. The attendees for the first session dribbled in over the next 45 minutes. Finally the class started. This scene was repeated throughout the next 4 days. People were in and out of the room, taking phone calls, answering pages, attending to other work-related details, etc. Needless to say, these people did not derive much from the training. When the system needed to be configured, they could not recall seeing the configuration settings although the trainer had done an excellent job in presenting those to the group. There is no doubt that this company should have sent their people to off-site classes.

The advantage to off-site classes is the hands-on, classroom instruction. People can concentrate on what the trainer is teaching them without interruptions or distractions. They can exchange ideas with other classmates on what phase of the implementation they are in, how they resolved problems with the system and other information. The disadvantage to off-site training is that the class is not structured for a specific company. It is also difficult to get questions that relate to a company's specific processes answered because there are people from a number of different industries in the same class. Those in attendance get a basic education on the system.

Companies must decide in which setting will their people derive the most from the training. Training is not cheap. It represents a sizable investment both in terms of time and money. Make sure that your people are given every opportunity to reap the benefits of this training.

Question: Why is it that ERP vendors do not teach the basic concepts of ERP systems?

Ellen: ERP vendors are first and foremost looking for companies who are in the process of changing or upgrading their legacy systems. ERP vendors want to sell their particular ERP solution and provide the services related to their particular solution. Many times, the individual who sells the ERP solution to a company is not the same individual who assists the customer with the system implementation or provides any training.

Many companies assume that the ERP vendor understands the basic concepts of ERP. The ERP vendor is looked upon as the 'expert' not only of the ERP software but also ERP concepts. While it is true that the ERP vendor is the 'expert' for their particular ERP package, often the vendor does not have a good understanding of the basic concepts of ERP.

There are many misconceptions about ERP. It is important that individuals understand what ERP really is, its impact on the business, how to manage the ERP implementation project, how to avoid disastrous project 'pitfalls', and how to maintain the ERP system after the 'go live' date.

CIBRES recommends that companies invest the time and money to make sure that their ERP core team and key users receive an educational class pertaining to ERP concepts. This type of training will prove to be an invaluable asset before, during, and after the implementation of their ERP system.

Ronnie: As strange as it may seem, it has been my experience that many of the ERP vendors really do not know the basic concepts of ERP systems and how business functions relate. They understand *their* software only and how their software performs.

Question: What should a company do when things are not going very well?

Ronnie: To quote William F. Halsey, "All problems become smaller if you don't dodge them, but confront them." Almost all projects of any size experience a period when things are not going well and it seems that no progress is being made. When this happens, a company should review the project and take steps to correct the issues hindering progress. The company should not give up and abandon the project. Project abandonment happens in many instances and the result is usually more costly than just the monetary value of the project. Credibility and confidence is lost if the project is abandoned.

When things are not going well, the company should take time to re-evaluate the situation and take steps to eliminate the problems and get back on track. In some instances the answer may be to seek assistance from an outside source, a "fresh set of eyes". Other solutions may be to review the real needs and expectations of the project. The company should review the tasks required and the amount of resources available. They should examine the areas of expertise of the available resources. Having plenty of resources is of little help if they are not the right resources. Support for the project and the project team should be very visible when things are not going well. Do not give the team reason to think it is being abandoned. On the contrary, the company should emphasize that the project was deemed important when it began and has not lost any importance. The company must have had a compelling reason to implement the change, so a few setbacks should not stop the project.

The project may run into many roadblocks along the way that will jeopardize the success of the project. Each time one of the roadblocks appears, actions should be taken to remove the roadblock or to find a way over or around the problem. The problems or roadblocks demonstrate the need for a strong project manager. When problems do occur, it is the project manager's responsibility to assemble the team members and find solutions. Sometimes the solutions are simple, other times not. If a project becomes bogged down with problems, consider an outside source as a means to the solution.

Projects that include regular project team meetings usually experience fewer unexpected problems. They identify the problems sooner and work out solutions. Review the project plan regularly to prevent the project from getting too far off course, thus resulting in serious problems.

Ellen: I agree, Ronnie; as with any project, events can happen that affect the success of the project. Unfortunately, despite a project manager's best efforts, a project can teeter on the brink of failure before anyone notices. This is especially true with an ERP system implementation because the project manager may also fill another position on the core team. When problems develop, the project should be halted.

The project manager should assemble the core team members, including management representatives. The purpose of the meeting is not to point 'fingers' at each other, the ERP vendor, or outside consultants. The focus of the meeting should be to discuss and resolve the issues.

The project scope should be reviewed. This will help the group to re-focus on what the company's original goals were. The project plan should also be reviewed. The project plan can provide a basis for determining the status of the project in terms of incomplete tasks, deadlines, required resources, and technical requirements. After a review of the project plan, it may be decided that simply adjusting the project plan may help to get the project back on track. All issues should be discussed and a resolution action plan developed. A method for resolving future issues should be established prior to the project continuing.

Even after doing all of the above, a company can still find that an ERP project may once again be in jeopardy. The project should be halted and the issues addressed. This may mean that the core team needs to be re-organized, an outside consultant may need to be hired to assist the project manager, or the project manager may need to be replaced with a 'heavy-weight' project manager.

A company should never allow a project to continue when it appears that the project is not progressing well. Failure to address these problems will cost a company in terms of time, money, and people. In some cases, a failed ERP project has meant financial disaster for certain companies. Do not allow a problem plagued project to continue – take action to correct any problems and get the project back on track.

Question: How often should the system be reviewed after the implementation?

Ronnie: As soon as the implementation is complete, it is time to re-evaluate. I know this may sound ridiculous, but remember, the average life of the system is 10-15 years. If the implementation took one year, the remaining life of your system may less than 9 years. CIBRES recommends that a company conducts periodic reviews at least every 5 years, but with technology progressing as rapidly as it is now, that may not be often enough. This does not mean that the total system will be obsolete or not functional or a that you will require a totally new implementation. It only means, you can not stop just because the project is "completed". Technology does not stop. It is moving forward at a faster rate than most companies can keep up with.

Napoleon Bonaparte once said, "One must change one's tactics every ten years if one wishes to maintain one's superiority." Every ten years might have been good enough then, but now the system should be reviewed more frequently. Your system should be reviewed for new requirements and demands that are being placed on the business, reviewed for new direction the company may determine to take. Can the system, as it is currently implemented, support the new long range business plans?

You must perform audits of the information in the system. Review the system for continued functionality fitting business needs. As part of the implementation project, the "new" system underwent a prototyping and testing phase prior to the "cut over". This prototyping and testing was performed to verify that the new system would perform adequately to fill the business needs. Now it is time to do it again. Test the system to verify it is performing in a manner that fits the current business processes and demands. Data was cleaned up and checked for accuracy prior to "going live". Now is time to do it again.

Remember, the project is never complete, ERP should be viewed as a never ending journey, not a destination.

Ellen: Yes, Ronnie, believe it or not, this is an area that many companies neglect. It is often assumed that once the ERP system is implemented there is no need to review the system. There are several phases that a company goes through when doing an ERP system review before the company can feel 'comfortable' with the flow of transactions within the system and the reports that are being generated out of the system.

Phase 1 – Prototyping and testing of the ERP system during the implementation is an integral part of the ERP project. This phase of the implementation is very important because it brings the capabilities of the software and the expectations of the company together. Many vendors refer to this as 'pilot' runs of the software. It allows the implementers of the system to test the software prior to the go 'live' date. This testing is critical for a smooth transition when the system goes 'live'.

There are several reasons why a company should prototype and test their 'new' ERP system. It provides a basis for making changes to the system prior to going 'live'. If the configured settings need to be changed, you can do this during prototyping and testing and then retest the settings for accuracy. A number of system and company process issues can be identified and resolved during this testing process.

During prototyping and testing of the system, definitive answers as to what the system will or will not do are learned. Prototyping and testing is an excellent learning tool for ERP teams to become familiar with the system. As individuals work through different processes on the configured system, ownership for the system develops.

Unfortunately, in their rush to implement the ERP system, prototyping and testing of the 'new' ERP system is often neglected. This can have detrimental effects after the system goes 'live'. It is much easier to address system concerns prior to the go 'live' than after. One executive commented that when his company tried to correct problems in the system after it was 'live', they found that it was similar to trying to keep an automobile on the road traveling at 100 MPH and not being able to take your foot off the accelerator.

Phase 2 – For a period of time after the system goes 'live', CIBRES recommends that the system be monitored for transaction flow errors, data entry standards, data entry errors, and report inaccuracies. If everyone did a 'good' job during the prototyping and testing phase these errors should be minimal. Testing and reviewing immediately following the go 'live' is something that every company must do. Some companies check the system every couple of hours at first, then once a day, once a week, etc.

Phase 3 – Once a company is relatively comfortable with the system and reports are deemed accurate, the company should develop a system review plan. Random checks of the system should be done to make sure that the transactions are flowing correctly and the data is accurate.

Phase 4 – It is a fact that an organization will change over time. Organizational growth, organizational structural changes, technology needs, and strategic business plans are all changes that can affect the ERP system's ability to meet the demands of the organization.

Reviewing the ERP system should be done at different stages of the system's life cycle. Organizations can approach these reviews at their discretion. Companies who have been successful with their ERP system monitor the system for performance issues, data integrity, and transactional process flows. They also perform evaluations to make sure that the ERP system can continue to support the organization's present and future growth.

Question: How does trust work with ERP systems?

Ronnie: Trust is essential for the success of the ERP system. Trust in the system must be developed and allowed to grow. Trust between management and employees must be maintained. Most system implementations require a great deal of change. Effective change management plays a key role in building and maintaining the trust necessary for a successful ERP system. Communication is essential in establishing and building this trust.

Effective change management is crucial to building and retaining trust. Change management could be a complete topic in itself. Employees have a tendency to resist change. Many are afraid of change. Some are fearful of losing their jobs. Others are afraid they will not be able to perform their functions effectively with all the changes. Most people are afraid to step outside of their comfort zone. That is why trust is so important. There must be trust that management has made the correct decision, trust that the new system will allow them to perform their functions, and trust that the new system is not intended to eliminate them from the company.

Even with good change management, trust in the new system must be established. People are usually comfortable with the old system, even if it included utilizing numerous subsystems to store information. With the implementation of the new system, how they store and retrieve information changes. The way they view information changes. Users must be able to trust that the information they obtain from the new system has the same integrity as that in the old system.

Trust must exist between users in different functional areas. An ERP system is an integrated system, thus each functional area relies on information or data that is provided by other functional areas. They must be able to trust that each area is sufficiently trained, trust that each area is performing their duties correctly, and trust that each area is accepting responsibility for ownership of their system. Management relies on information from the system to make business decisions. With such high stakes, trust is essential.

Ellen: An ERP system is an integrated business tool. It is a business tool that is used by all the functional areas of a company. For example, customer information entered by the sales department is shared by accounting, production, and distribution. It is also a people system. It is the people who must use and maintain the system. The integration of an ERP system 'tears' down the traditional walls between the functional areas. The system forces departments to communicate with each other regarding the ERP system. Where distrust might have existed before, trust begins to be built between the functional areas.

Users of the system must trust that each functional area will maintain their system responsibilities. The receiving department must trust the purchasing department to maintain the purchase order module so when items are received they can process the receipt of the item in the system. The accounting department must trust the receiving department to process the receipt so they can enter the vendor's invoice and process it for payment.

Everyone within the company must be able to trust the data that is in the system. Inventory, bills of material and routings should be 99% accurate at all times. Of course, this requires that data standards, controls, and procedures be established for maintaining the data. There should be no doubt that the information contained in the system is correct. When people can not trust the system data, islands of manually maintained information will begin to 'crop' up in the company.

Management must be able to trust the financial reports being generated out of the system. These financial reports are used by management to make decisions for the organization, address organizational issues, gain a competitive edge in the market, and analyze trends.

The modular, integrated design of an ERP system promotes trust within an organization. If trust is lacking, the ERP system will soon begin to disintegrate. Data integrity problems will appear. Management and others will not use the ERP system because they do not trust the data or reports. Trust is one of the critical success factors of an ERP system.

6

How does one measure the success of an ERP system? This is a question that many companies fail to ask. Companies that have poor measurement systems remain unaware of the disruptions to their business. Those that have well development measurement systems can respond quickly to changing needs. There are many characteristics for measuring the successful use of an ERP system. Having good measurement systems helps companies identify and fix problems before they become disruptive to their business. Measurement systems revolve around the people, processes, and technology of ERP systems.

In this chapter the reader will learn...

1. What are some warning signs?
2. How does a company measure technology?
3. How does a company measure business processes?
4. How does a company measure people?
5. What is data integrity?
6. What is the CIBRES scorecard system?

Question: What are some of the warning signs that the ERP system or implementation is in trouble?

Ronnie: 60% to 80% of all ERP system implementations are in danger of failure or, once implemented, fail to provide the expected results. Seldom do implementations fail or systems perform inadequately without some advance warning that something is wrong. Too often, companies fail to recognize the warning signs or fail to take action once the warning signs become evident. Some of the most common warning signals that an ERP system or implementation is in trouble are:

- Negative attitudes within the organization,
- Data integrity problems,
- Long processing times,
- Unresolved technical issues, and
- Strained relationship with the ERP vendor.

Negative attitudes toward the implementation are very damaging to the progress and success of the project. All efforts should be made to prevent or to eliminate negativism as soon as it surfaces. Even after implementation, negative attitudes toward the new system will greatly hinder the use and success of the system. If top management develops a negative attitude toward the system, the attitude can kill the implementation or doom the system even after implementation.

Unresolved technical issues, if left unresolved, will eventually stop or kill the project.

Long processing times add to the frustration of the users and will feed the negative attitudes if not addressed in a timely manner. Long processing times may be a result of underestimating the size requirements of the hardware needed to handle the amount of traffic with the new system.

Problems with data integrity, if left unaddressed, can kill an implementation or render a system useless after implementation is complete. Data integrity problems feed the negative attitudes toward the system. Information obtained from the system is viewed as worthless. Subsystems begin to be developed by the users to obtain, record, and maintain the information they need to perform their functions. The use of these subsystems can result in a vicious circle. Time is spent obtaining, recording, and maintaining information in the subsystems, resulting in less time available to identify and correct root causes of the data integrity problems, thus resulting in increased data corruption.

Ellen: Yes, Ronnie, and you know, just as a person develops symptoms when becoming ill, an ERP implementation project has warning symptoms that it's not well. These symptoms can develop at any time during the implementation of the ERP system. Some companies develope symptoms before the ERP solution is even purchased. Let's look at some of these warning symptoms.

Symptom #1 – A negative organizational attitude can not only jeopardize the success of the implementation project but also cause the 'death' of the ERP system. It's important that a company addresses this issue quickly. One manner for dealing with this is for senior management to let everyone know that they are 100% committed to the successful completion of the project. They are supporting the ERP project manager and core team. This gives the project credibility and makes it 'real' to others within the organization.

Symptom #2 – During an implementation, it's not uncommon for strained relationships to develop between the ERP vendor and the company. More often than not, the vendor is blamed when the project goes over budget, is not completed on time, or does not live up to the expectations. Many times, it is not the vendor who is at fault. The company has not taken ownership of the project or the system. Deadlines are not being met. Users have not been properly trained. Procedures and controls are not in place to support the system. Documentation is missing.

Symptom #3 – Data integrity problems should be viewed as big 'red' flags that the ERP system is not well. Remember that the ERP system is a business tool that must be managed and maintained by the people. If bad data is downloaded into the system, this bad data will produce inaccurate reports. Lack of data standards can lead to data integrity problems. If no one is responsible for maintaining the accuracy of the master records, such as bills of material, the system will develop data integrity problems.

There are other symptoms that may develop to signal that an ERP system is in trouble. If these occur during the implementation project, the project should be stopped. A meeting of the ERP core team should be assembled, the issues discussed, and resolutions determined. If these warning signs are not handled quickly and promptly, they will continue to escalate.

A company must keep its 'finger' on the pulse of the ERP system. Warning signs need to be dealt with and not ignored. Ignoring the warning signs will not make them disappear; they will continue to be a problem long after the ERP system is 'live'. These warning signs can prove to be such a source of frustration to management and users that the system is never fully utilized.

Question:	I have heard that the people, processes, and technology must all work together to create a successful ERP system. Can you tell me a little more about that?
Ellen:	The successful implementation of an ERP system is dependent upon a support structure consisting of people, processes, and technology. A company will have difficulty implementing an ERP system if any one of these elements is missing. Companies that take the initiative to make sure that their people, processes, and technology are aligned with their ERP system, have a much better chance of a successful implementation than companies that do not consider these important elements.

People – People must take ownership of the ERP system. It is their system. People enter data, perform data maintenance tasks, perform system maintenance tasks, etc. People's unwillingness to take ownership of an ERP system is a serious problem. A company can not afford to let this symptom go unresolved. Without people support, the ERP system will degrade and cease to provide any useful information to management.

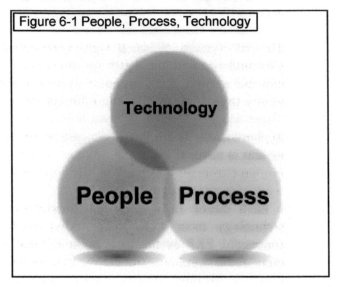

Figure 6-1 People, Process, Technology

Technology

People   Process

Processes – Every company has its own manner of conducting business. It is important that the ERP system be in alignment with the business processes of the company. Companies need to have a clear understanding of their business processes prior to selecting an ERP solution. Many companies purchase an ERP system without doing an analysis of their current business processes. They do not consider the company's future business goals. As a result they often purchase an ERP solution that lacks the functionality needed to run their business.

A company has only two options when it comes to an ERP solution and their business processes.

Option 1 - Adapt their business processes to the business process flows of the software.

Option 2 - Customize the software to accommodate their business processes.

The second choice is the least recommended. Customization of the ERP solution can be very expensive, time consuming, and can affect the ability to upgrade the system in the future.

Technology – There have been many advances in technology over the past few years. When implementing an ERP system, the company should have a clear understanding of their technology plan. Is the company planning to extend the ERP solution out to their customers and vendors via the Internet? Are they planning on implementing bar coding for warehouse inventory management? Do they need to interface EDI with the ERP solution? Does the company require a 24/7 operation?

These are some of the technology issues that a company should answer prior to starting an ERP implementation. It is most unfortunate when companies do not take the time to do a technology plan and then find that the ERP system will not accommodate their future plans.

Successful implementation of an ERP system requires the alignment of people, processes, and technology. These make up the supporting structure of the ERP system. Failure to include any one of these in the implementation project can mean disaster to the ERP system.

Ronnie: You are so right about that, Ellen. Now let me further explain the correlation. People, processes, and technology can be viewed as an equilateral triangle, each side being a critical part of the ERP system. This triangle is applicable to the successful implementation of the ERP system as well as the ongoing success of the system. All three elements are of equal importance; without either of the three, the implementation and the system will fail to meet desired expectations.

For implementation purposes, the people side focuses on the type of implementation team approach that is to be used, i.e. the lightweight, heavyweight, functional, or A Team. These different approaches describe the make up of the project team, with special emphasis on the type of project leader being utilized. After implementation, the continued success of the system depends on people, particularly the end users. The users must take ownership of the system. The success of the system depends heavily on the satisfaction level and the confidence level of the users. The proper training and education of people is necessary to obtain the most benefit from a system. Without people accepting ownership of the system, the system will suffer a painful death.

For implementation, the processes relate to the implementation strategy to be deployed, either the big bang, phased, parallel, hybrid, or process. Each of these strategies has advantages and disadvantages. No one strategy can be classified as better than the other; the type strategy and successful use of that strategy is dependent on the company culture, expectations, and preparation.

For post implementation, the processes relate to the business function flows. How does the business operate? What is the workflow, flow of information and data, and methods used within the organization? Each company has its own culture, its own business requirements, and different demands for functionality. Meeting the processes or business needs is the intended goal when selecting software to be implemented. Future demands and requirements on the business must be included in the considerations when selecting a system.

The technology side of the triangle relates to the software and hardware that is used for implementation and support of the people and processes after implementation. Technology changes constantly. It is important for enterprises to be aware of the new trends and developments in technology but it would be impossible to implement every new technology on the market. Knowing what is available and staying abreast of the changing technology is critical. Advances in Internet capabilities continue to provide increasing opportunities for e-business and e-commerce. What demands, both now and in the future are the company going to place on the system? That question requires much consideration. The answer will have a major effect on the type software and hardware selected.

Question: How do we measure our processes?

Ronnie:

Cibres

The *"ERP: A-Z Implementer's Guide for Success"* contains the entire scorecard system. CIBRES item number 4516.

A good source for information relating to identifying and measuring the processes, people, and technology of the company is the CIBRES scorecard system, a free service of CIBRES, and can be viewed online at www.cibres.com. The TQM, Continuous Improvement, and JIT sections, and the Operational Set-up, Planning, and Control sections are most relevant to measuring your processes. The education and training section also includes questions relating to the process of education for the employees. The scorecard can be completed in its entirety or by sections that are deemed relevant.

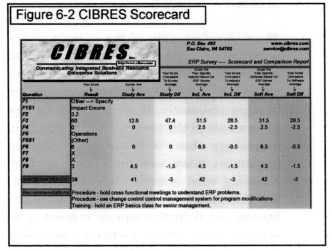

Figure 6-2 CIBRES Scorecard

The performance measurement section of the scorecard provides measurement for key performance areas such as inventory accuracy, on time shipments, supplier deliveries, routing accuracy, bill of material accuracy, percentage of orders shipped complete, and master production schedule accuracy. The Sales and Operations

Planning process should be measured for its accuracy and results.

Tracking and tracing are two methods used in the scorecard to measure processes. These methods are similar, utilizing the ability to connect records and follow transactions to identify problems in the processes. Once the problems are identified, analysis is done and solutions are implemented to correct the problems.

Ellen: I agree, Ronnie, and you know, an ERP system integrates and automates many of the tasks that people perform during the course of a business day. Whether it's entering a new sales order, scheduling a job to fill the order, shipping the order, or invoicing the customer, all the information necessary to complete the sales process is available to everyone. If the sales process is followed, the customer's order should be delivered as promised; but what happens when the order is not delivered on time? Where did the process 'break' down? Was it a system error or a problem with the company's business process?

This is an example of an event that can occur and disrupt the normal business process flows. ERP systems come with a variety of tools that help a company measure their processes to find the root cause of these types of problems. Tracing, tracking, date stamps, menu logging, and history logging are some of these tools.

Tracing is a methodology for connecting 2 records that have something in common. Using drill down capabilities of the system and following the links between these 2 records can help find where a problem occurred. Tracing is based on the principle of newest to oldest record.

Tracking is often confused with tracing. Tracking is similar methodology except it is based on the principle of oldest to newest records.

By analyzing the records, the 'break' down in the process can be identified. These types of problems can usually be attributed to human error rather than system errors. It is a recommended best practice that companies establish a quality assurance plan for their ERP system.

Question: How do we measure our people involved with ERP? What areas? What types of measurements?

Ellen: An unauthorized user logs into the ERP system and modifies the bill of material used to produce an item. An order is received for the finished item. MRP is run and purchasing is notified that raw material needs to be ordered. Purchasing orders the material. The material is received – only to be discovered that the wrong material was ordered. As a result, the customer is unhappy because his or her order is not delivered on time. It's the system's fault that this happened; or is it? How can a company find out what happened?

ERP systems have history logging capabilities. History logging is a methodology that records all additions, deletions, and changes that were made to the database records. By checking the history log, a company can review all the activity associated with the record, including who changed the record and when it was changed. The history log file can be a valuable tool when problems need to be identified.

Menu logging is another tool that can be used. Menu logging tracks the activity of a user as they move from one menu to another within the system and shows all menus and options that a user selected.

The menu logging and history logging capabilities of the system can be used to help a company identify unauthorized changes to database records. Menu and history logging can help to identify users who try to access portions of the system that they do not have the authority or rights to access. These tools can be used in conjunction with other security tools to make sure that the users are not abusing their system privileges.

Ronnie: The CIBRES scorecard system, that I mentioned before, provides a free online diagnostics tool with measurements for the people involved in ERP as well as the areas to be measured. People involvement can be measured in relationship to their participation in the project as well as use of the system. The areas that can be measured include team structures and participation, education and training, communication, and reward systems as well as user related items such as accuracy of information input by the user.

As Ellen mentioned, an ERP system has history logs, date stamps, time stamps, etc. that contain information that will allow users to be measured on the number of transactions performed, menus viewed, time spent on the system, etc.

Question: How does a company measure the technology? How do we know if we are keeping up with technology?

Ellen: Unfortunately, most companies do not measure their technology systems unless a system failure occurs. IT may not realize there is a problem unless they start getting complaints from the users of the system. Some of those complaints may include speed required to access the database, poor response time when trying to enter data, or applications that 'lock' up.

There are many diagnostic and troubleshooting tools that companies can use to monitor their technology equipment. Some of the areas that companies frequently monitor are system performance levels, CPU usage, or RAM.

Many companies enlist the assistance of outside professionals to help them measure their technology. These agencies can help the company assess their current technology capabilities and put together a technology improvement plan.

It's important that companies monitor all of their technology requirements. One company I know had a very extensive plan in place to monitor all of the servers in the organization. Management wanted to make sure that the servers and network were functioning 24/7. A detailed disaster recovery plan was also implemented. Despite all of their careful planning, someone had neglected to include a single PC that was sitting in the shipping area. Since it was a stand-alone unit, management and IT did not perceive it as a problem. This PC was used exclusively for processing bar-code labels that a major customer required. The company could not ship any product without the appropriate bar-code label on the carton. The PC 'died'. As a result, the company lost $250,000 in sales. This was a very expensive learning experience for the company.

Companies need to pay attention to their technology. CIBRES recommends that an IT budget be planned so that money is allocated for the maintenance and upgrading of equipment. Normally, an IT budget should be based on .5% to 2% of a company's yearly revenue figures.

Ronnie: Also, Ellen, companies can use the CIBRES scorecard system to measure the technology they use against the technology available. Companies should examine the available technology such as email, use of the Internet, introductions of new software, upgrades to their existing software, etc. Companies should not only find if a technology is available, but also measure how the technology is used. For example, is email being used effectively?

Companies should monitor and measure system utilization. Processing speeds, volume of transactions, number of users, average user activity, number of database lockups, etc. can and should be measured to see if the system is meeting its expectations.

Continuous review of the current system and new products available on the market will assist companies in determining whether they are keeping up with technology. Some companies enlist the services of outside sources to evaluate their systems against new and future technology. Most IS departments budget for upgrades and for new technology tools.

Question: What is the CIBRES scorecard system?

Ellen: The CIBRES scorecard is a free online assessment tool for ERP systems. It provides a means for companies to measure how their ERP software, people, and processes compare to other industry averages. This tool can help companies identify the problems, take corrective actions, and put preventative measures in place.

The scorecard is divided into sections. These sections contain a series of questions that the company needs to rate (0-10). Environmental characteristics, initial decision criteria, project management, people systems, and strategic planning are examples of the sections contained in the scorecard. Companies can select which sections they want to rate; however, CIBRES encourages them to complete all sections so that their company can receive a comprehensive overall report of their ERP system and functional activities.

You can access the CIBRES scorecard by visiting the CIBRES organization website and clicking on the ERP Scorecard button. You will be presented with an overview of the scorecard, instructions, and a listing of the sections that you may access. You will need to fill out the contact information so the scorecard results and comparison report can be emailed back to you. Remember that there is no charge for accessing the online scorecard or receiving the comparison reports by email.

After answering the questions, you will receive the results of the scorecard in the form of a comparison report. The report will include detail line item results, sectional scores, averages of all participants, industry averages, software averages, recommendations, and notes. This report can help you identify weak areas of your ERP system. You can then decide how to correct these problems by implementing a process improvement plan for your ERP system.

Often companies realize that they have problems with their current ERP system but are unable to identify the root causes of the problems. As one executive said, "We know we have problems with our ERP system but we don't know how to identify the problems. You can not resolve issues without first knowing what the issues are. It's like being in a maze and not being able to find your way out". With the CIBRES scorecard companies can identify these problems and their root causes. The more effort a company 'puts' into answering the questions, the more comprehensive the comparison report will be. It can take a few hours or several weeks to receive the report back, depending on the number of questions that are answered.

The CIBRES scorecard is a valuable tool for any company who wants to improve their ERP system and processes. CIBRES recommends that all companies take the time to answer the questions that pertain to their company needs, receive the report, and put a corrective plan into action. You should remember that your ERP system is not just a piece of software but an enterprise-wide solution that needs to be managed as effectively as possible. The CIBRES scorecard is a tool that can help companies do just that – manage the enterprise.

Ronnie: Let me add, Ellen, the time required to input the answers to the complete survey is approximately two hours. However, you should spend time preparing the answers in advance to get a more accurate picture of your ERP system. Results are emailed (unless specified otherwise) and contain the standard scorecard and comparison reports.

The Scorecard results and the Comparison Report is designed to provide information to assist companies in indentifying weak areas in their ERP system. The Scorecard contains scores by section, and details of each line item result. The comparison report provides statistics that allow companies to see how their system is performing compared to averages in the industry, averages for software, as well as comparable averages to other companies that participate in the use of the scorecard. Another benefit contained in the results is the recommendation and notes section.

Question: What are key areas for measuring data integrity?

Ronnie: I think often of a quote from a former general manager of mine, "Without data it is only an opinion, without actions, data is useless ..." I often change the last part of the quote to, "without integrity, data is useless." Most enterprises consider financial data to be the most critical information they require. For this reason, any data that influences the financial data should be audited for correctness. Customer and product information is also critical.

Any file or record containing cost information should be audited for accuracy. The item master or part master file normally contains the cost information associated with an item. These costs may be reflected as actual cost, standard cost, last purchase price, going to cost, etc. The cost used depends on the accounting method utilized by the enterprise, LIFO, FIFO, actual, standard, etc. The going to cost field is usually used when preparing for a new cost roll-up or a change in cost. Depending on the system setup, these costs will drive the valuation of inventory.

One of the most critical items for data integrity is inventory accuracy. Inventory information affects the stated value of assets, drives requirements for expenditures for materials, drives requirements for production, and affects the enterprise's ability to satisfy customer requirements. Inventory accuracy is more than just the correct number of items in inventory. Inventory accuracy includes count, part number, description, storage location, and the assigned value (regardless of costing method).

In a manufacturing or assembly enterprise, bills of material and routing accuracy is a key area to be measured. The BOM contains the component part number and the quantity of each component required to produce a product. BOMs containing inaccurate data will result in inaccurate cost information and component requirements. Inaccurate BOMs may also result in a product being produced incorrectly. Routings contain the steps, the sequence, and the resources required to produce a product. This information is utilized for capacity resource planning as well as costing. Inaccurate information will distort the cost of the product, may cause delays in producing the product, and in some instances result in unusable product.

Vendor, customer, and employee data are three other critical areas for data integrity but are often overlooked. Incorrect or insufficient information such as phone numbers, contact names, ship to addresses, bill to addresses, and email addresses may result in poor communication, inaccurate billings, and frustrated vendors or customers. Inaccurate employee information may result in under or overpaying the employee, inaccurate withholding of deductions for the employee, and may create problems when attempting to contact employees.

Much emphasis is and should be placed on training users to properly use the system, to take ownership and responsibility for the system, thus taking responsibility for the accuracy and integrity of the data. However, there are other factors that influence data integrity. For example, bugs in the software that do not allow the system to function as it was meant to perform. Viruses that may creep into the software, especially systems that utilize Internet capabilities. Hardware failure, especially while processing transactions, can corrupt the database.

Ellen: Data is one of the key elements of an ERP system. When a user inquires on the stock status of an inventoried part, there should be no doubts that the data is accurate. If users cannot trust the data in an ERP system, they will cease to use that data. The integrity of the data should never be an issue.

Let's examine some of the ways in which data integrity can become corrupted. Human error represents the biggest threat to data integrity. People must enter data into the system. Wrong keystrokes or misinformation can be entered. The company may not have data entry standards set; therefore, everyone enters the data, as they perceive it should be entered. Lack of data entry standards can compromise the integrity of the data, which often leads to duplicate records within the master database files.

Data that is transmitted from one computer system to another can cause data problems. A popular ERP solution recently moved from a FoxPro database structure to a SQL database structure. When existing customers tried to convert the data over to the SQL structure, massive data corruption problems occurred. This was in part due to the fact that the customers neglected to maintain their data properly. Another means for transmitting data is electronic data interchange (EDI) and downloading files off of the Internet.

Software bugs, viruses, hardware equipment failures, and natural disasters can all affect the integrity of the data within the databases.

There are ways that a company can minimize the risk of data corruption and protect the integrity of the data. Establish data entry standards. For example, make sure that everyone knows how to format the data that is entered into customer, vendor, inventory, and BOM master records. Control access to the data through security, such as passwords. In most ERP solutions, the system administrator can set up security and block access to fields that appear on screens for users. User interfaces within the ERP solution can also be set up to detect invalid data before it is saved in the database. Some of these interfaces are hard coded into the ERP solution but there is also the ability to soft code certain configuration settings that act as filters for invalid data entries. There are several commercially produced software packages that a company could use to detect and correct data inaccuracies prior to loading it directly into the ERP system. Many companies use these detection software packages when they are receiving data via EDI to screen for data problems before it goes into their ERP systems. Anti-virus software is also a tool that can be used to detect any computer virus that may corrupt the data. Last but not least establish a disaster recovery plan that includes regular daily backups of the data.

An ERP system that is plagued with 'bad' inaccurate data becomes a frustrating, useless business tool to a company. Management can not trust the financial reports; purchasing can not trust the inventory reports; sales can not trust customer and order information; and the list goes on. Don't let this happen to your ERP system. A little prevention and planning will ensure that the integrity of the data is protected.

Question: What are some of the common mistakes that companies make when purchasing or installing an ERP system?

Ellen: A number of errors that companies make when purchasing or implementing an ERP system comes from a lack of understanding the basic concepts of ERP. Many senior managers do not view the ERP system as a business tool that will be used to 'run' their entire organization. As a result of this thinking, many companies choose their ERP systems based on what another company is using, an advertisement, a magazine article or just because it sounds like it'll do the 'job' for them. Unfortunately, this usually proves to be a very costly mistake.

Some people believe that a company's success comes from software. However, a company's success comes from the management of its resources – people, money, and time. The ERP system is only a business tool that provides management a means to manage those resources.

Many companies think that the bigger the ERP software package the better it will perform. They may decide to purchase an Oracle or JD Edwards solution without giving any thought to the skills needed to maintain the system. For example, a small conveyor belt manufacturer purchased an Oracle solution. No one in their IT department had any experience with Oracle. It took them over three years to implement just a portion of the system. When the CEO was asked if he would make the same choice again, his answer was an emphatic, "NO!" He compared it to a man wearing an overcoat three sizes too big. Bigger is not necessarily better if the ERP solution does not 'fit' your company.

Another misconception is that an ERP solution will correct all of the company's problems. In talking with companies and management, this seems to be the number one reason why they want to change software. A company can purchase the best ERP system in the world, but if its processes, procedures, controls, and resources are not managed, the software won't keep the company viable.

Many companies can be successful in choosing their ERP solution and implementing an ERP system if they plan the ERP project by following proven system selection and implementation methodologies.

Ronnie: You are exactly right, Ellen. Purchasing and installing an ERP system for the wrong reasons is one of the most common mistakes companies make. "Everyone else is doing it so it must be the right thing to do". "The competition did it". But does a real need exist within the company? There should be a compelling reason to undertake a project the magnitude of an ERP implementation.

Undersizing or oversizing the software being purchased and installed is another common mistake. Some companies use the "one size fits all approach". Often the thought process is that the bigger the software, the better it will operate and the more it will help. Another misconception is that it costs more so it must be more valuable and provide more benefits. Other companies make the mistake of choosing a smaller package, usually because of cost factors such as initial cost and installation. Either oversizing or undersizing can result in horrendous results. Purchasing a software package without sufficient testing of the software, checking of references, and modeling of the software to fit the business needs is a mistake that is made too often.

Lack of consideration of hardware requirements is a very common mistake. Can the current hardware support the new software? Will additional terminals, desktops, printers, bar coding equipment, scanning equipment, etc. be required to operate the system or to get the full benefits from the implementation? These requirements are often initially overlooked, then result in project cost over-runs.

Failure to establish a project team and develop a project plan is another very common mistake. Some companies' approach to selection, purchase, and installation of new software is to give it to the

IS department. Most often, this is a huge mistake. Even companies that form project teams do a poor job of selecting team members and project leaders, most often selecting whoever is available regardless of qualifications or expertise. The need for outside assistance such as consultants is not recognized until the project is in trouble.

Ellen, I'm sure you will agree when I say that inadequate education and training is the one common mistake that I would classify as the most common, yet most costly mistake companies make. Too often, there is little or no education provided. If education is provided, it is commonly limited to a select few, and these are usually the wrong few. Proper training in the use of the new system is essential, yet many companies view training as providing little value. Users will "learn as they do" philosophy is prevalent in these cases. Proper training includes all users of the system, not just data entry individuals. Among companies that do provide training, it is common for them to fail to train the proper people. Too often, the supervisor or lead person in an area is trained in the proper use of the system, but they fail to train the actual every day user.

These are only a few of the common mistakes companies make. Over the years I have seen many variations to these mistakes, but they all usually end with the same miserable results.

As you read these questions and answers, I would like to encourage you to not become disillusioned with the concept of ERP and what it can do for your enterprise. ERP is a magnificient tool that can be used to assist in improving your business. It takes a lot of hard work. But with proper planning and execution of the plan, ERP can be implemented successfully and you can reap many benefits. I feel assured the information provided in this publication will be of assistance to you.

Other CIBRES Publications (www.cibres.com)

Visit the CIBRES Website for the latest publications and services of the CIBRES organization. Same day shipment on almost all educational materials, certification exam registrations, interesting articles on ERP, list servers, diagnostic tools, seminar registrations, and the latest news!

"ERP: A-Z Implementer's Guide For Success" represents the most comprehensive textbook in the history of ERP systems. It has 20 chapters with about 750 pages packed with full color diagrams, figures and charts that explain basic concepts common to all ERP systems.

It has been chosen by the CIBRES.COM organization as the primary study textbook for the CIERP certification, a professional certification for ERP professionals. Each chapter contains questions at the end to challenge the student. Case studies from actual implementation experiences provide insight on how companies manage and use ERP systems. It has quickly become the worldwide desk reference selling in over a dozen countries. No ERP professional, implementer, executive, manager, or organization should be without this important desktop reference.

www.cibres.com